HOW TO
STOP
BURNOUT

"If you feel burnout setting in, if you feel demoralized and exhausted, it is best, for the sake of everyone, to withdraw and restore yourself"

Dalai Lama

Introduction

How are you?

Fine?

Isn't that the answer we are taught to give?

People would ask me how I was doing, and I'd give them the standard answer.

"I'm good. Things are going well, and all is good."

It wasn't.

The problem was that I didn't realize it until I was empty, exhausted, and burnt out.

The sad news is that it's a familiar tale. As a society, we are more stressed, medicated, and burnt out than at any time in history. We are overworked, overcommitted, and overwhelmed.

If you're reading this book, you are probably staring at deadlines, attempting to eat healthy, stay fit, keep up with friends, care for your families, and juggle a thousand other things. All the while, you hope you can make it to the end of the day without someone asking something of you.

Does that sound familiar?

If it does, then you are not alone. It's the story of millions of people, and it's my story. I was the overwhelmed guy desperately trying to hold it all together. I've been there, done that, and have the stress-induced grey hairs to prove it.

"How to Stop Burnout" is the self-help book I needed. It's a guide about getting you to wave goodbye to burnout. It has practical, actionable advice you can use, not just smile and nod at. This book will cut through the clichés and quick fixes to offer you genuine strategies that don't suck for stress relief and self-care. Because let's face it, saying stopping burnout in the chaos of professional and personal life isn't just good, it's essential.

Who's this for, you ask? If you're constantly on the go, dealing with the pressures of work, family, and life, and looking for a no-nonsense way to find some peace, you're in the right place. You're driven, seeking balance, and open to self-improvement–as long as it doesn't involve chanting on a mountain somewhere.

Skeptical? Good. You should be. A landfill of self-help books is out there promising the moon and the route to nirvana. This is a different kind of book. We won't sugarcoat it: This journey is long and hard but achievable and worth it.

We will discuss boundaries, mindfulness, self-care, to-do lists, and some affirmations. Yeah, I said it. Hear me out before you roll your eyes and toss this book out the window. We're not talking about the "look in the mirror and tell yourself you're a strong, beautiful unicorn" kind. We're diving into affirmations that punch hard, resonate with your gut, and make sense in your world–the kind that acknowledges life can be a dumpster fire, but you've got the extinguisher.

Consider this book your roadmap from burnout to living a more peaceful life. We'll explain why you're stressed, how it's messing with you, and how different techniques can make a world of difference.

So, what do you say? Are you ready to drop the pretense, open your mind, and give this a shot? Let's kick burnout to the curb, find some peace, and get you where you can enjoy your life.

CHAPTER 1

THE STATE OF PLAY

"Burnout is a real risk, especially now when there is so much news. I take real breaks, put my phone down, get out into the countryside, and ignore the news
- even if it's just for a few hours."
Katty Kay

In a world where our inbox never sleeps and our phone buzzes like it's possessed, it's easy to wear the "busy" badge with honor. Until, one day, the weight of it threatens to overwhelm you. It sneaks up on you, doesn't it? One minute, you're powering through your to-do list like a boss, and the next, you're staring at your computer screen, wondering if you are about to have a stress-induced meltdown. It's the modern dilemma: balancing the hustle with the need to stay sane. So, how do you tell the difference between working hard and being one step away from burnout?

1.1 Recognizing the Signs of Overwhelm

What is burnout?

Burnout is more than just feeling tired or stressed; it's a state of chronic physical and emotional exhaustion often accompanied by feelings of cynicism, detachment from work, and a sense of ineffectiveness or reduced accomplishment.

Does that sound familiar?

Burnout is commonly used in the context of workplace stress. Maslach and Leiter (2016), pioneers in burnout research, define burnout as a psychological syndrome emerging as a prolonged response to chronic interpersonal stressors on the job. They conceptualize it as having three main components:

Emotional Exhaustion: Feeling drained of emotional resources, being emotionally fatigued, and finding it challenging to face the demands of the job.

Depersonalization (Cynicism): Developing negative, cynical attitudes and feelings about one's job, clients, or colleagues, leading to a sense of detachment.

Reduced Personal Accomplishment: Experiencing a decline in one's feelings of competence and achievement at work, often accompanied by decreased work-related efficacy.

Burnout has been widely studied in various professions and industries, recognizing its impact on individuals' mental and physical health, job performance, and overall well-being. It can result from a combination of factors, including high workload, lack of control over one's work, unclear job expectations, and insufficient support from colleagues or superiors.

There have been several times when my work was so stressful that it bled into my personal life and led me on the path to burnout. When I reflect on those jobs, I see that they tick all the boxes outlined in the research. It's easy to spot the problems with hindsight, but what if you're currently working a stressful job?

Awareness is key

It starts with that fifth cup of coffee you're downing to make it through the afternoon or that third night in a row when you're bringing work to bed. Physical symptoms like tension headaches that make you feel like there's a vice around your skull or that irritable edge in your voice (the one that makes your dog think twice about asking for a walk) are glaring neon signs.

Emotional red flags? They're there, too. Maybe you're snapping over small stuff or feeling that heavy chest of dread as the weekend draws closer. I had one job where my family would start to avoid me on Sunday night because my mood changed, anticipating the 8 am Monday meeting. Your body and mind are waving a flag, signaling it's time to slow down.

Stress vs. normal pressure

Not all pressure is the enemy. That adrenaline rush from a last-minute deadline or the buzz after nailing a presentation? That's your body's way of rising to the occasion. But when the hustle stops feeling like a rush and starts feeling like you're running from a bear 24/7, it's time to reassess. Stress can be more than just a nuisance, especially the kind that digs in its heels. It can mess with your health, happiness, and how you show up in the world.

The role of self-reflection

Some stress triggers don't announce themselves with a headache or yelling at traffic. That's where a bit of quiet comes in handy. No, you don't need to sit cross-legged and hum (unless that's your jam), but taking a few minutes for some good old-fashioned self-reflection can work wonders. Whether journaling your thoughts at the end of the day or taking a mindful moment in the morning to set your intentions, getting to know your stressors is like detective work for your well-being.

Early detection

Imagine if you could catch stress the way you see that typo in an email – before it goes out. Recognizing those early signs of stress means you can manage it before it manages you. It could be noticing when your sleep starts to go off the rails or when your patience is thinner than your morning pancake. This isn't about avoiding stress altogether – let's face it, that's about as possible as avoiding traffic in the city. It's about knowing your signs and having your strategies ready to roll.

In the dance of daily life, it's all too easy to step into the rhythm of constant busyness. Recognizing the signs of overwhelm is the first step in changing the music to something more peaceful. With awareness, distinguishing healthy pressure from harmful stress, engaging in self-reflection, and catching those early signs, you're setting the stage for a life where you're in control – not your calendar, boss, or whatever social media tells you to be.

1.2 The Myth of the "Busy Badge of Honor"

In a world where the length of your to-do list measures your self-worth, it's no wonder we're all sprinting on the hamster wheel of busyness. But here's a radical thought: What if I told you that being perpetually busy isn't the trophy we should strive for? Let's pull back the curtain on society's busyness pageant and see it for what it is–a mirage of success leaving us exhausted.

Cultural glorification of busyness

It's everywhere, from the brags about back-to-back meetings to the hustle culture noise on social media about working weekends. Busyness has become the status symbol of modern-day life. It's as if the more you have on your plate, the more important you must be.

Let's get real. Busyness is not a badge of honor; it's a ticking time bomb. This glorification of constant activity doesn't lead to success or happiness; it often leads to the opposite. It's time we question the narrative and consider there's more to life than being busy.

Busyness as a stressor

Let's say it out loud: Constant busyness isn't just a harmless trait of the highly ambitious. It's a significant stressor, and it'll wreck your life. Your mind doesn't have time to relax when you're always on. This can lead to burnout, a state of emotional, physical, and mental exhaustion caused by prolonged stress. It's like running your car engine in first gear, full throttle, non-stop. Eventually, something's going to give. The trick isn't to keep pushing harder but to find balance. It's about making time for work, play, and rest. Because when you're burned out, nothing's getting 100% of you–not your job, not your family, and certainly not yourself.

Redefining productivity

How do we break free from the cult of busyness? It begins with redefining what productivity means. True productivity isn't about how much you can cram into your day but how effectively you use your time to achieve what matters most to you. Enter mindful productivity. This concept is all about being present and intentional with your tasks. Instead of multitasking into oblivion, it's focusing on one thing at a time. Mindful productivity values quality over quantity, and it recognizes that rest and recharge time are not just nice to have; they're essential for sustained performance. It's about working smarter, not harder, and remembering that you're a human being, not a doing.

Practical de-escalation techniques

Are you feeling the weight of the world on your shoulders? It's time to lighten the load with some practical de-escalation techniques. These are your tools to step back from the brink of overwhelm and reclaim your calm.

Priority check: List all the tasks vying for your attention. Be brutally honest about what needs to be done today versus what can wait. This simple act of prioritizing can take a load off your mind.

The power of "no": Saying no to extra commitments that don't serve your goals or well-being is not selfish; it's necessary. It frees up space for what truly matters.

Technology detox: Set designated times to unplug. Whether during meals, an hour before bed, or Sunday afternoons, stepping away from screens can drastically reduce stress.

Mindful breaks: Integrate short, mindful breaks into your day. Five minutes of deep breathing, walking around the block, or just stepping outside for fresh air can reset your stress levels.

Routine reshuffle: If your current routines contribute to your sense of busyness, it's time for a reshuffle. You could batch similar tasks, set specific times for email checking, or delegate what you can. Small changes can lead to significant improvements in how you manage your day.

The shift from glorifying busyness to embracing mindful productivity isn't just about getting more done. It's about creating a life that feels good on the inside, not one that just looks good on the outside. It's about recognizing that you have nothing to prove by running yourself ragged. Instead, it's finding strength in stillness, power in pause, and success in simplicity.

So, let's take the busy badge of honor, set it on fire, and toss it into the sea. It's not helping you; it's leading you towards burnout. It's time to redefine what it means to be genuinely productive, to work in a way that sustains our energy and ignites our passion rather than depletes it. Here's to finding your version of peace in the chaos, one mindful step at a time.

1.3 Stress and Its Disguises in Daily Life

Life's not always about the big stressors; sometimes, the tiny grains of sand slowly fill your shoes, making each step more uncomfortable than the last. We need to watch out for these small, stealthy stressors. They sneak in unnoticed, under the guise of "just another day," but cumulatively, they can utterly overwhelm you.

Hidden stressors

Think about the last time you couldn't find your keys, as you were already running late, or when you hit every red light while in a rush. Annoying, right? Now, imagine these minor annoyances happening day in and day out. Individually, they seem trivial, but their power lies in their persistence. These hidden stressors are part of your daily routine, lurking in the underbrush of your busy life. They're the constant background noise you've learned to tune out, not realizing the slow drip of stress they're injecting into your system.

The cumulative effect of minor stressors

Here's the thing about these tiny irritants–they accumulate. Like fat clogging an artery, these small sources of stress build up over time, significantly impacting your mental health and well-being. It's not the deadline at work that's the tipping point; it's also the spilled coffee, the missed workout, and the forgotten lunch combined. This accumulation can lead to constant overwhelm, where you're always playing catch-up with your life. The key is not to let these minor stressors compile unchecked.

Mindfulness in daily activities

You've probably heard about mindfulness, but before you dismiss it as something that requires sitting silently for hours on end, consider this: mindfulness brings awareness to the present moment, whatever that moment entails. It's about noticing the warmth of the water as you wash dishes, the feel of the air as you walk outside, or the flavor of your food as you eat. When applied to daily activities, mindfulness can help you identify those hidden stressors by making you more aware of your reactions to seemingly mundane events. This awareness is the first step in transforming these moments from stress-inducing to, at the very least, neutral experiences.

Mindful driving: Instead of cursing every red light, pause to take a few deep breaths, notice the tension in your body, and consciously relax your grip on the steering wheel.

Mindful eating: Turn off the TV, put away your phone, and focus on your meal. Notice the textures, flavors, and sensations of eating. It's not just about enjoyment; it's about turning a daily necessity into a stress-reducing activity.

Mindful listening: In conversations, practice focusing entirely on the other person without planning your response while they're still talking. This improves relationships and reduces the stress of misunderstandings and conflicts.

Creating a stress-minimized lifestyle

The goal here isn't to eliminate stress–that's about as feasible as emptying the ocean with a teacup. Instead, focus on strategies to reduce and manage these hidden stressors effectively. It's about making minor adjustments to your daily routines to mitigate the accumulation of stress, allowing you to navigate your day more efficiently and less tense. Streamline your morning routine: Lay out your clothes, prep your breakfast, and pack your bag the night before. Reducing morning chaos can have a ripple effect on your entire day.

Organize your space: A cluttered space can contribute to a cluttered mind. Spend a few minutes each day tidying up. This isn't about a spotless home but about creating an environment that doesn't add to your stress.

Schedule downtime: Just as you schedule meetings and workouts, block off time in your day for relaxation and leisure. Treat this time as non-negotiable, a necessary component of your stress-minimized lifestyle. Set boundaries with technology: Designate tech-free times, particularly before bed, to reduce the stress associated with constant connectivity. Use this time to engage in activities that relax and recharge you.

Adjust your expectations: Be realistic about what you can achieve in a day. Setting the bar too high can lead to a constant feeling of failure and frustration. Celebrate your accomplishments, no matter how small. In weaving these practices into the fabric of your daily life, you're dodging stress bullets and changing the game. It's about shifting from a reactive stance, where stress controls your day, to a proactive one, where you navigate your day with intention and awareness. This doesn't require monumental changes but relatively small, deliberate actions that gradually steer your life toward calm. By addressing the hidden stressors in your daily routine, you're laying the groundwork for a lifestyle that supports your well-being, allowing the peace you seek to emerge naturally.

1.4 The Impact of Stress on Physical Health

When stress kicks in, your body isn't just idly standing by. Nope, it gears up as if it's about to face off with a saber-toothed tiger. This fight-or-flight response is your body's old-school way of keeping you alive in the face of danger. It's handy when there's an actual threat, but not so much when the 'threat' is an overflowing inbox or a traffic jam.

The body's stress response

Imagine your body as a high-tech security system, always on the lookout for potential threats. The moment it senses stress, it sounds the alarms—hormones like adrenaline and cortisol flood your system. Heart rate? Up. Blood pressure? Sky-high. It's prepping you to either fight or run from danger. This is useful in the short term, but things start to go haywire when your body's in constant red alert mode.

Long-term effects

So, what happens when the "danger" doesn't let up, and your body's alarm system is stuck on high alert? Chronic stress becomes a squatter in your body, contributing to a laundry list of health issues. Heart disease, for starters, doesn't just spring up out of nowhere. High blood pressure and increased heart rate over time can wear out your heart, making you a prime candidate for cardiovascular woes. And diabetes? Stress has a hand in that, too. Constant cortisol spikes can mess with your blood sugar levels, paving the way for Type 2 diabetes.

Let's remember the hit your digestive system takes. Have you ever had that gut-wrenching feeling when stress is at your door? That's not just an expression. Stress can lead to everything from heartburn to irritable bowel syndrome. And your sleep? Forget about it. Stress is the ultimate nightmare that keeps you tossing and turning, which feeds into the cycle of stress. It's like your body's twisted version of a "gift" that keeps giving.

Stress and the immune system

Your immune system is like your body's bouncer, keeping intruders at bay. But when stress occurs, it's like your immune system has had a few too many, slacking off and letting its guard down. The result?

You're susceptible to everything from the common cold to more severe infections. And if you've ever wondered why you always catch a cold when you're burned out, now you know. Stress is rolling out the red carpet for illnesses.

Holistic stress management

Alright, enough doom and gloom. There's light at the end of this stressed-out tunnel, and it's all about a holistic approach to kicking stress to the curb. This isn't about slapping a Band-Aid on a bullet wound; it's about getting to the root of the problem and giving your body the support it needs to bounce back.

Get moving: Exercise isn't just about getting skinny or shredding for the summer. It's one of the most effective ways to burn off that stress-induced energy. Whether it's hitting the weights, going for a run, or dancing like nobody's watching, find something that gets you moving and stick with it. Your heart, brain, and stressed-out self will thank you. Eat smart: Food is critical, especially when managing stress. Ditch the junk food that sends your blood sugar on a rollercoaster ride and opt for whole, nutrient-rich foods. Think fruits, veggies, lean proteins, and whole grains. They're like premium fuel for your body, helping it run smoothly even when stress is trying to gum up the works.

Sleep it off: Never underestimate the power of a good night's sleep. Turn your bedroom into a cool, dark, and quiet sleep sanctuary. And put the phone down an hour before bed. Your emails can wait until morning, but your health can't.

Mind over matter: Techniques like meditation and deep breathing aren't just for Zen masters. They're tools in your stress-busting toolkit, helping to calm your mind and bring your body's stress response down a notch. Even a few minutes a day can make a difference.

Connect: Humans are social creatures, and isolation only feeds into stress. Lean on your friends, family, or even a furry companion. Sometimes, knowing you're not alone can lighten the load.

Laugh: Never underestimate the power of a good laugh to break the tension. Find reasons to laugh, whether it's a comedy show, a funny podcast, or just messing around with friends. It's a natural stress reliever that reminds you not to take life too seriously.

Stress might be a fact of life, but being overwhelmed by it doesn't have to be. By understanding how stress affects your body and adopting a holistic approach to managing it, you're not just surviving but thriving. It's about creating a lifestyle that supports your physical and mental well-being, letting you live with a little more ease and peace.

1.5 Mindfulness: The Antidote to Automatic Stress Responses

Mindfulness has become the buzzword of the century, floating around like a cure-all prescription for the modern world's ailments. But strip away the hype; what you're left with is remarkably simple and profoundly effective. At its core, mindfulness is about being fully present in the moment, engaging with our experiences, thoughts, and feelings without judgment. It's the opposite of running on autopilot, where reactions are more about habit than choice. This shift from mindless reactivity to mindful response is where the magic happens, especially regarding stress management.

Understanding mindfulness

Let's break down why mindfulness is the big deal everyone makes it out to be. Imagine a stressful workday: emails are piling up, deadlines are looming, and your phone won't stop buzzing. The automatic response? Your heart races, frustration builds, and maybe you snap at a colleague or two. Here's where mindfulness steps in. The pause button lets you step back, assess the situation, and choose how to respond rather than letting your stress response call the shots.

Mindfulness vs. autopilot

On the surface, life on autopilot might seem efficient–going through routines and tasks without much thought. But it's a double-edged sword. While it can help manage the daily grind, it also means you're less aware of the stress building up until it's too late. Mindfulness flips the script. It's about tuning in rather than tuning out, noticing the little things that add up to how you feel at any moment. When you're mindful, you're in the driver's seat, aware of your stress triggers, and able to navigate them with intention.

Practical mindfulness exercises

So, how does one start practicing mindfulness, especially during a hectic day? The beauty of mindfulness is its simplicity and accessibility. You don't need special tools or settings; you just need a moment and a willingness to try. Here are a few exercises that can slot right into your daily routine:

Focused breathing: This is mindfulness 101. Take a minute or two to concentrate solely on your breath. Inhale deeply through your nose, feel your chest and belly rise, and then exhale slowly through your mouth. This simple act can center your thoughts and lower stress levels almost instantly. There are excellent guided meditations online that will help you through this.

Sensory grounding: Use your senses to anchor yourself in the present. Identify five things you can see, four you can touch, three you can hear, two you can smell, and one you can taste. It's a quick way to bring your focus back to the now, cutting through the noise of stress.

Mindful eating: Turn a meal or snack into a mindfulness practice. Eat slowly, savor each bite, and consider the flavors, textures, and sensations. It's not just about enjoying your food more; it's about breaking the cycle of mindless eating and stress.

Walking meditation: Next time you walk, whether it's to a meeting or just around the block, make it a meditative experience. Pay attention to the rhythm of your steps, the feel of the ground beneath your feet, and the sounds around you. It's a way to clear your head and get a fresh perspective.

Building a mindfulness habit

Incorporating mindfulness into your daily life doesn't have to be another task on your to-do list. Start small and build from there. Here are some strategies to make mindfulness a natural part of your routine: Set reminders: Use your phone or a sticky note as a cue to take mindful breaks throughout the day. It could be as simple as a deep breathing exercise or a quick check-in about your feelings.

Link mindfulness to daily activities: Attach a mindfulness practice to something you do daily, like brushing your teeth or waiting for your morning coffee to brew. These regular routines can become triggers for a mindful moment.

Be patient with yourself. Mindfulness is a skill, and like any skill, it takes practice. There will be days when it feels impossible to focus or when you forget to practice altogether. That's okay. The key is to keep at it without judgment.

Find a mindfulness mate: Having a friend or colleague interested in practicing mindfulness can be a huge motivator. Share tips, experiences, and reminders to encourage each other.

Keep it flexible: There's no one way to practice mindfulness. What works for one person might not work for another, and what works for you one day might not work the next. Be open to experimenting with different practices and find what fits best into your life.

In the modern world's hustle and bustle, mindfulness offers a rare respite to slow down, tune in, and manage stress on your terms. By making mindfulness a daily practice, you combat stress and enhance your overall quality of life, one present moment at a time.

It's also vital for me to say this: If you feel you are approaching burnout, you must speak to someone qualified to help. A medical doctor or licensed therapist would be great people to connect with. Don't struggle alone.

CHAPTER 2:

BOUNDARIES

"You have to love and respect yourself enough to not let people use and abuse you.
You have to set boundaries and keep them, let people clearly know how you won't tolerate to be treated, and let them know how you expect to be treated."

– Jeanette Coron

A key lesson to learn in the journey to stop burnout is establishing and maintaining effective boundaries. Imagine your life as a garden. Your time, energy, and peace of mind are the precious plants growing within it. What happens when every bug and weed thinks it's an all-you-can-eat buffet? Chaos ensues. Your once serene garden becomes overrun, your prized peonies trampled, and your tomatoes, well, let's just say they've seen better days. This is what happens when boundaries are more suggestion than law in the land of your life. It's not about building a fortress but installing a good fence and deciding who and what gets the time of day. And the good news is you can do this without an ounce of guilt.

2.1 The Importance of Boundaries

Boundaries are the lines we draw around ourselves to protect our mental garden from getting trampled. They clearly demarcate "this is okay" and "Not a chance." Why are they crucial? Without them, it's like leaving the gate wide open. Anything and everything can waltz in, taking a piece of your peace of mind, your time, and sometimes even your self-worth. From the coworker dumping their tasks on you to the friend who treats you like their 24/7 therapist, boundaries keep you from becoming the world's doormat. Plus, they're fundamental to healthy relationships. They help you respect others and teach them how to respect you.

Overcoming Guilt

Ah, guilt, the unwelcome guest that shows up whenever you try to say "no." It whispers, "You're being selfish," or "A good friend would say yes." I've had all of these said to me. However, setting boundaries is

21

not selfish. It's self-preservation. When you're clear about your limits, you're better than everyone around you because you're not stretched thinner than a dollar store t-shirt.

Acknowledge the guilt: Recognize it's there, but don't let it be the boss of you.

Reframe your thinking: Instead of "I'm letting them down," think "I'm taking care of myself so I can be my best for those around me."

Start small: Practice saying no to more minor things. It's like building a muscle. The more you do it, the stronger it gets.

Practical Steps to Setting Boundaries

Let me be honest with you - setting boundaries was a struggle for me, and it took me a while to get comfortable with the whole idea. Saying "no" felt like I was signing up for consequences, especially since I'd seen people ostracised, demeaned, and sidelined because they had started setting boundaries. Prioritizing your health over what others want might rub some folks the wrong way, and that's okay. Your well-being matters more than what people think. Sadly, in the real world, bosses and even friends sometimes push us to the brink just to get what they want. It's a harsh reality we've got to navigate.

Here are some simple, straightforward ways to set boundaries.
Identify your limits: Sit down and think about what stresses you out or makes you uncomfortable. These are your no-go zones.

Communicate clearly: Don't hint or beat around the bush. Be direct about what you can and cannot do. "I can't take on extra work this week," beats "I'm not sure I have the time."

Offer alternatives: When you can, offer an alternative. "I can't help with this now, but I can tackle it first thing next Monday."

Stick to it: Consistency is critical. The more you stick to your boundaries, the more others will respect them.

The Role of Self-Respect

Setting boundaries is a form of self-respect. It's you saying, "My time, energy, and well-being are important." You reinforce your values to yourself and others whenever you uphold a boundary. It's not just about saying no to others but saying yes to yourself—to your peace, sanity, and right to tend your garden how you see fit.

So, there you have it. Boundaries are not barriers but the framework that allows you to grow, thrive, and enjoy the garden of your life. They're not about pushing people away but about nurturing your well-being so you can engage with the world more fully and freely. Remember, a well-tended garden isn't selfish. It's a thing of beauty, a source of nourishment, and a place of peace. And that's something worth guarding.

2.2 Prioritizing Self-Care Over People-Pleasing

Have you ever found yourself saying yes when every fiber of your being screams no? That's the people-pleaser in you, working overtime. The only thing you're scared of is letting people down.

Identifying People-Pleasing Behaviors

Recognizing you're a people-pleaser isn't always easy, especially when your knee-jerk reaction to asking to do something is "yes." It's like trying to read the label from inside the bottle.

Try asking yourself these questions:

Am I the go-to person for everything, even when it's not in my job description or my responsibility?

Does "No" feel like a foreign word that gets stuck in my mouth, and I must summon the courage to say it?

Do I feel guilty for even thinking about putting my needs first? Is there always someone else that I feel needs to come before me?

Am I juggling tasks like a circus performer, all because I can't bear the thought of someone being disappointed?

Does this sound familiar? Well, you're not alone. Many of us fall into the people-pleasing trap. I used to think it was the only way to be liked, accepted, or get ahead in my career.

The Cost of People-Pleasing

This constant need to please comes with a price tag, and it's not just your sanity on the line. The toll is hefty:

Emotional burnout is because you're always on and accommodating. Physical exhaustion because, surprise, constantly bending over backward isn't great for your health.

Your needs and wants get pushed so far down the list that you lose sense of yourself.

And here's the harsh reality: all this effort to make everyone else happy doesn't guarantee they'll like you more. It's like running on a treadmill, hoping to get somewhere. I've worked for bosses who will take everything they can from you, and the moment you are too exhausted to carry on, they will ditch you on the side of the road. It's time to get off the treadmill.

Self-Care Strategies

Self-care isn't selfish; it's survival. Here's how to start treating yourself like someone worth taking care of:

Schedule me-time: And no, scrolling through your phone doesn't count. I'm talking about time blocked off just for you, doing something that refills your cup. It could be reading, hiking, or just staring at the ceiling, contemplating the meaning of doughnuts. If it's on the calendar, it's real.

Learn to love "no": Think of "no" as "yes" to yourself. It's not about being a jerk but being honest about what you can and can't do. People will respect you more for it, trust me.

Get physical: Exercise isn't just for your body; it's a mental escape hatch. Find something that makes you feel good, and do it regularly. Your brain will thank you.

Mind your mind: Meditation, deep breathing, or just five minutes of doing nothing can do wonders for your mental state. It's like giving your brain a mini-vacation.

Assertiveness Training

Being assertive doesn't mean you're suddenly donning a villain's cape; it means respecting yourself and others enough to communicate honestly. Here's your training regimen:

Start small: Practice assertiveness in low-stakes situations where the outcome doesn't keep you up at night. It could be sending back a steak that's more rubber than ribeye or asking a neighbor to kindly turn down their midnight opera sessions.

Use "I" statements: "I feel," "I think," "I need." It's not about blaming; it's about owning your feelings and expressing them clearly.

Stay calm: Keep cool, even if the other person gets heated. Think of yourself as a duck: calm on the surface, paddling like hell underneath. Repeat as necessary: Sometimes, you must sound like a broken record before it clicks. "As I mentioned, I can't take on that project right now." There you have it. Escaping the people-pleasing trap isn't about turning into a hermit or a heartless automaton. It's about finding balance, respecting yourself, and realizing that you can't pour from an empty cup. So, go ahead and make yourself a priority. The world won't fall apart, I promise. Instead, you'll start experiencing it in technicolor because everything else seems brighter and more doable when you care for yourself. And that, my friend, is the real victory.

2.3 The Ripple Effects of Saying "No"

When you start viewing "no" not as a rejection but as a redirection of your energy, the effects ripple out, touching every corner of your life like the first drop of rain on a still pond. It's more than just a shield against the onslaught of demands; it becomes a beacon guiding you toward a more authentic, fulfilling life. Let's peel back the layers on this, shall we?

Positive impacts on personal life

What if commitments no longer hijack your weekends? Instead, when you choose where your "yes" goes, you're suddenly at the helm of your free time. Your hobbies collecting dust and the family adventures on the back burner are now front and center. Stress starts to peel away, layer by layer. You're no longer a human doing; you're a human being, fully present in your moments of joy and relaxation. It's like finding an extra day in the week, a hidden treasure where you reconnect with what lights you up inside.

Effect on relationships

I used to think that saying "no" would push people away and close doors to me. And I was right; it did. But it pulled other people closer and opened different doors for me. As it turns out, the people it pulled closer were people with great boundaries who avoided burnout and thrived in their lives. These are the people I wanted to be closer to. The doors that opened to me would not lead me to burnout but to exciting and fresh possibilities.

Setting boundaries is like handing out a map of your life, showing others where they are welcome and what areas are off-limits. This doesn't just breed respect; it cultivates a deeper understanding and appreciation between you and your people. Conversations move from superficial chit-chat to meaningful exchanges. Your relationships transform into these robust structures, resilient against the storms of misunderstanding and resentment. It's no longer about pleasing everyone; it's about enriching your connections with authenticity.

Improved professional life

In your professional life, "no" becomes your secret weapon for productivity and satisfaction. Think about it: when you're not buried under a pile of "yes"-induced projects, you can focus on what you're good at, maybe even passionate about. This isn't about slacking; it's about strategic selection and choosing tasks that align with your strengths and goals. The outcome? Your work quality skyrockets, deadlines stop feeling like death sentences, and that elusive work-life balance? Suddenly, within reach. Your boss sees someone who delivers top-notch results, not because you're clocking in more hours, but because you're investing your hours wisely. It's a win-win; the company gets the best version of you, and you get to reclaim your sanity.

2.4 Reclaiming Your Time and Energy

In the maze of daily commitments, it's easy to find yourself sprinting on a treadmill set to "ludicrous speed." You're moving, sure, but are you going anywhere or just burning out? It's high time we talk about managing the finite resources you've got: time and energy, not in the old, worn-out way that makes you feel like you're failing Time Management 101, but in a way that feels like you're finally playing the game with cheat codes.

Time Management Techniques

Here are some tactics to wrangle your calendar back under control without making it feel like a straitjacket.
Batching tasks: Group similar tasks together to tackle them in one focused sprint. It's like doing laundry: whites with whites, colors with colors. It saves time and energy.
Saying no: Already covered, but worth repeating. Your time's a VIP section, not a free-for-all concert.

Tomato Time Management

The Pomodoro Technique is a time management method developed by Francesco Cirillo in the late 1980s. It's named after the Italian word for "tomato," as Cirillo initially used a tomato-shaped kitchen timer to track his work intervals. The technique improves focus and productivity by breaking work into short, timed intervals separated by brief breaks.

Here's how the Pomodoro Technique typically works:

Choose a Task: Select a task you want to work on.

Set the Timer: Set a timer for 25 minutes (this interval is often referred to as one "Pomodoro"). During this time, you focus exclusively on the task at hand without any distractions.

Work on the Task: Concentrate on the chosen task until the timer rings. If you think of something else you need to do during this time, jot it down on a piece of paper, but return to your task immediately.

Take a Short Break: Take a short break (usually around 5 minutes) when the timer goes off. Use this time to stretch, grab a drink, or do something unrelated to work to relax your mind.

Repeat: After the short break, return to your task and start another Pomodoro (25 minutes of focused work). Repeat this cycle until you've completed four Pomodoros.

Longer Break: After completing four Pomodoros, take a more extended break, typically 15-30 minutes. Use this time to recharge before starting another set of Pomodoros.

The Pomodoro Technique helps improve productivity by breaking work into manageable intervals, providing a structured approach to work, and regular breaks to prevent burnout. It also encourages focus by minimizing distractions during each Pomodoro.

While the traditional Pomodoro interval is 25 minutes, some people may find that shorter or longer intervals work better for them. The technique can be adapted to suit individual preferences and tasks. Additionally, many Pomodoro apps and timers are available to help implement the method effectively.

Energy Audit

Now for a bit of detective work: an energy audit. It's not about your electric bill but figuring out what in your day gives you a boost and what drains you.
Keep a log: For a week, jot down activities and rate them on an energy scale. At one end, you have vampires, which are activities that suck the life from you. At the other end of the scale are batteries, which give you energy. You must understand what is happening with the energy in your life.
Notice patterns: Do certain people light you up while others leave you deflated? Is there a time of day when you're unstoppable? Data is power.

Eliminating Energy Drainers

Now you are armed with your energy audit, it's time to prune. This isn't about a ruthless cull but about making smart choices about where your energy goes.

Delegate or ditch: Some tasks just aren't worth your vibe. If you can, hand them off. If not, question if they're essential.

Limit exposure: For energy-draining folks, limit the time spent in their company. Think of it as emotional sunscreen.

Refine routines: If morning emails zap you, switch them up. Rearrange your day to play to your strengths.

Investing in Energy Boosters

With some newfound free time and energy, reinvesting wisely is crucial. This is about doubling down on what makes you feel like you've got a turbo button.

Lean into passions: More time for hobbies means more joy. Whether it's woodworking or salsa dancing, make it a priority.

Connect: Spend time with people who make you laugh, think, and feel alive. It's soul food.

Rest and recharge: Never underestimate the power of doing nothing. Sometimes, the best use of your time is to simply rest.

Managing your time and energy isn't about squeezing every drop out of every minute. It's about making those minutes count, filling them with the stuff that lights you up, and tossing aside the stuff that dims your shine. It's not rocket science, but it takes a bit of honesty, courage, and willingness to do things differently. And the payoff? A life that feels richer, fuller, and decidedly more fun.

So, as you move forward, keep these principles in your back pocket. Play around with them, tweak them to fit your life, and watch as the days start to feel less like a mad dash and more like a leisurely stroll. After all, isn't that the point? To enjoy the journey, not just race to the finish line.

Empowerment and confidence

Now, for the grand finale: how saying "no" is a turbo boost for your self-confidence and sense of empowerment. Every time you stand your ground, it's a victory, a small rebellion against the tyranny of the urgent and unimportant. It proves you value yourself, your time, and your well-being enough to protect them. You know that you are worth it.

This isn't a one-off; it's a habit, a muscle that grows stronger with every use. You start to see yourself as capable and worthy of respect and consideration. It's not arrogance; it's assurance, a deep-seated belief in your worth that radiates out, affecting how you see yourself and others. You're no longer at the mercy of external demands; you're steering your ship, navigating through the waters of life with a newfound confidence that comes from knowing you have the power to choose.

So, there you have it. Saying "no" isn't just about turning down requests; it's about saying "yes" to a life lived on your terms. It's about reclaiming your time, enriching your relationships, excelling in your career, and building a rock-solid sense of self. The effects of this simple word ripple out in ways you might not expect, transforming not just your present but shaping a future that looks a lot more like the one you've been dreaming of.

Share Your Insights, Change a Life. Embrace the Joy of Helping Others

"Kindness is the language which the deaf can hear and the blind can see."
- Mark Twain

People who extend a helping hand without expecting anything in return often find deeper fulfillment in life. So, if we have the chance to make a difference together, let's seize it.
To kickstart this journey, I
have a simple question for you...
Would you lend a hand to someone you've never crossed paths with, even if no one knew it was you?

Who is this someone, you wonder? They're much like you—or at least, how you used to be—eager to navigate life's challenges, seeking guidance but unsure where to find it.

My mission is to ensure that How to Stop Burnout reaches everyone who needs it. Every effort I make is rooted in this mission, and the only way to achieve it is by reaching... well... everyone.

This is where you come in. As it turns out, most people judge a book by its cover (and reviews). So here's my humble request on behalf of a struggling soul in our shared journey:
Please consider leaving a review for this book to assist those grappling with burnout.

To experience that heartwarming sensation and truly make a difference, all you need to do is... in less than 60 seconds...leave a review.
Simply scan the QR code below to share your thoughts:

If the thought of aiding a stranger resonates with you, then you're my kind of person. Welcome to our community. You're among friends.

I am genuinely thrilled to guide you through strategies to combat burnout in the upcoming chapters. Trust me; you'll find them invaluable.

Thank you, sincerely, for considering this request. Now, let's resume our journey toward a more balanced and fulfilling life.

With utmost gratitude,

Patrick Clarke

CHAPTER 3

HELLO SUNSHINE

"Morning is an important time of day because how you spend your morning can often tell you what kind of day you are going to have."
– Lemony Snicket

When I look back on my spiral into burnout, I see something alarming. I would wake up stressed. My alarm was like a warning siren that set me up for a terrible start to the day. As I set out to stop burnout, I realized I had to change my morning routine and become deliberately mindful.

Imagine waking up with a sense of calm anticipation for the day ahead. It sounds like a scene straight out of a Disney movie. Well, it's more attainable than you think. The secret? It's all about how you kick off your day. Picture the morning not as a frantic race against the clock but as a sacred space for setting the tone of the coming hours. That's the power of a mindful morning. It's not about doing more; it's about doing differently. Here's how to transform those first groggy steps out of bed so you can face whatever the day throws at you calmly and clearly.

3.1 The Power of a Mindful Morning

My morning routine was familiar to many people. The alarm goes off, and I groan, hit snooze, roll over, and wait for it to sound again. I finally drag myself out of bed, and then it's a mad dash to get out the door. It was stressful for everyone around me and set me off for a terrible start to the day.
I had to flip the script.

Imagine starting your day grounded and centered, with a clear mind and a relaxed body. That's the gift of infusing mindfulness into your morning routine. It's like putting on armor for the day ahead, but it makes you feel lighter and more agile instead of weighing you down. This doesn't require waking up at dawn for hours of meditation. It's about weaving mindfulness into the fabric of your morning, turning routine actions into moments of awareness and intention.

Creating a Morning Routine

Let's get practical. Transforming your morning starts with intention. Here are some simple steps to weave mindfulness into the start of your day:

Wake up with gratitude: Consider one thing you're grateful for before opening your eyes. It could be as simple as the comfort of your bed or the fact that you have another day ahead. Starting with gratitude shifts your mindset from "I have to" to "I get to."

Silence the screens: Resist the urge to dive into emails or social media. Give yourself the gift of a screen-free start, even just for the first 15 minutes. This creates space to tune into yourself, not the outside world's demands. One of my best mindfulness decisions was leaving the phone downstairs and buying a cheap alarm clock.

Mindful hydration: Begin your day with a glass of water. As you drink, do so mindfully, paying attention to the sensation of the water, its temperature, and the way it feels going down. It's a simple act but a way to anchor yourself in the present.

Mindful Movement

Gentle exercise in the morning does wonders, not just for your body, but for your mind too:

Stretch it out: Spend a few minutes stretching your body. Pay attention to each movement, how it feels, and where you're holding tension. It's not about pushing yourself; it's about waking up the body with kindness. Go for a walk: This gets the blood flowing, lets sunlight in your eyes (except during the Irish winter), and offers all the benefits of exercise.

Breakfast with a Presence

How often do you eat breakfast while scrolling through your phone, barely tasting your food? Let's change that:

Sit down to eat: Make it a point to sit at a table, not stand at the counter or, worse, eat over the sink.

No distractions: Keep the screens off. This is a time to be with your food and yourself.

Savor each bite: Pay attention to your meal's flavors, textures, and aromas. Chew slowly, appreciating the nourishment you're providing your body.

Gratitude for your meal: Take a moment to express gratitude for your food, the hands that prepared it, and the nourishment it offers you.
Starting your day with mindfulness is about something other than adding more to your morning to-do list. It's about doing what you already do with intention and awareness. It's the difference between gulping down life and savoring it, one moment at a time. And the best part? These practices are free of extra time or special equipment. They require you to show up, be fully present, and be ready to start your day calmly and clearly.

So, as you open your eyes to the new day tomorrow morning, remember: you have the power to set the tone for the hours to come. Choose mindfulness, and watch how it transforms your mornings and your entire day.

3.2 Mindful Commuting: Turning Traffic into Tranquility

So, you've rolled out of bed and feel peaceful from your new mindful morning routine, but now comes the real test–the commute. For many, this is the gauntlet, a daily ordeal filled with honking horns, jammed trains, or endless red lights. But what if I told you that the commute could be more than a stress-fest? Believe it or not, it could be a golden hour for mindfulness.

Reframing the commute

I used to hate commuting. I dreaded the inevitable traffic jams and would shout at other drivers the whole way to the office. It was stressing me out, and for no reason. I had to change my mindset. Instead of viewing it as a necessary evil, a chunk of your day lost to whoever designed the shocking road system, I started to see it as me-time.
Whether you're driving, cycling, or riding public transport, this chunk of the day is yours. It's a buffer between home and work life, a space where you can gear up in the morning or wind down in the evening. The trick is to shift from seeing it as time wasted to time gifted.

Mindful listening

Instead of trying to drown out the world or passively letting a podcast wash over you, choose what you listen to with mindfulness in mind.

That might be calming music that helps center your thoughts. It could be an inspiring, uplifting podcast. I found the news would stress me out or depress me, so instead, I would play the most optimistic music I could find. That helped me walk into work smiling and leave the stress far behind.

The key is active listening. Engage with what you're hearing. Reflect on it. Let it spark ideas or bring you a sense of peace. This active engagement makes the commute a part of your mindfulness practice rather than just transitioning from point A to B.

Breathing exercises

Breathing. It's something we do all the time without thinking. But when done with intention, it can be a powerful tool for stress relief. And the best part? You can do it anywhere, anytime–even in the middle of bumper-to-bumper traffic or squeezed into a train carriage. Here are a couple of techniques to try:

The 4-7-8 technique: Inhale deeply through your nose for a count of 4, hold that breath for a count of 7, then exhale slowly through your mouth for a count of 8. This method is a tranquilizer for the nervous system, perfect for when the commute tests your patience.

Square breathing: Imagine tracing the sides of a square with your breath. Inhale for a count of 4, hold for 4, exhale for 4, and hold again for 4. This rhythmic pattern can help bring a sense of order and calm to chaotic moments.

These exercises aren't just about filling time; they're about returning to your breath, to the present, and finding a calm center within the commuting storm.

Observation games

Lastly, let's talk about keeping the mind engaged and present. Ever find yourself zoning out during the commute, only to snap back to reality and realize you've arrived at your destination with no memory of the journey? It's common, but there's a way to counter it. Try these simple observation games to maintain mindfulness:

Count the smiles: It might sound cheesy, but it works. Look around and count how many people you see smiling. It's a way to connect with the humanity around you, shifting focus from the negatives to the positives. Find the color: Pick a color each day and then see how many times you can spot it during your commute. It's a simple way to keep your mind focused on the here and now rather than drifting into worries about the day ahead or the day behind.

The detail game: Choose an object—maybe a building you pass every day or the interior of the bus or train car—and try to notice five new things about it. This game is about seeing the familiar with fresh eyes, fostering a sense of curiosity and wonder.

Turning your commute into a time of mindfulness is about paying attention to the reality of traffic jams or crowded trains. It's about finding peace within that reality, discovering pockets of tranquility amid chaos. It's a way to build resilience and start and end your day with a sense of calm and presence that you carry with you long after reaching your destination. So tomorrow, as you step out the door and into the fray, remember. This commute could be the most unexpectedly joyful part of your day.

3.3 The Power of Present-Moment Eating

Pause for a second. When was the last time you tasted your food? Not just chewed and swallowed while your mind raced through your to-do list, but truly savored every bite? If you're scratching your head trying to remember, it's time to bring mindfulness to the dining table. Eating, an act as old as time itself, hides a golden opportunity to slow down and connect with the present.

Eating mindfully isn't about fancy foods or perfect settings; it's about fully experiencing what's on your plate. It's the antidote to the autopilot eating that happens when you're munching on a sandwich while scrolling through emails or snacking in front of the TV. By paying attention to eating, you're inviting a sense of gratitude and appreciation for the nourishment provided, turning a basic need into a rich experience.

Elevating digestion: As the saying goes, your stomach doesn't have teeth. Mindful eating aids digestion by encouraging slower chewing and thorough enjoyment of each bite. It's simple: the more you chew, the easier it is for your body to break down food, leading to better nutrient absorption and less digestive discomfort.

Heightening food enjoyment: Ever wolf down a meal and then wonder where it all went? Mindful eating flips this on its head. By focusing on your food's flavors, textures, and aromas, you're not just eating; you're indulging in a sensory experience. This heightened awareness can make the most straightforward meal feel like a feast for the senses.

Regulating appetite: Mindful eating aligns with your body's hunger and fullness cues. When you eat slowly and with intention, you give your body time to signal when it's had enough, reducing the likelihood of overeating. It's a kinder approach to managing your appetite and can be a helpful ally in maintaining a healthy weight.

Mindful Eating Techniques

Transforming mealtime into a mindfulness practice is easier than you think. Here are some practical steps to get you started:
Chew slowly: Make a conscious effort to chew each bite thoroughly. This will aid digestion and allow you to thoroughly taste and appreciate your food.

Eliminate distractions: Turn off the TV, put down your phone, and step away from the computer. Dedicate your full attention to eating, making it a distraction-free zone.

Engage all your senses: Before you take the first bite, take a moment to look at your food, smell its aromas, and anticipate its flavors. This sensory engagement can turn the most straightforward meal into a rich experience.

Check-in with yourself: Throughout the meal, periodically pause to assess your hunger and fullness levels. This helps you stay attuned to your body's signals and makes it easier to stop eating when you're comfortably full.

Creating a Mindful Eating Environment

The environment in which you eat can significantly influence how mindfully you consume your meals. Here are a few tips for creating a space that encourages present-moment eating:

Designate a dining area: Eat at a table rather than on the couch or desk. This helps reinforce the idea that mealtime is a distinct, important part of your day.

Minimize clutter: A cluttered dining area can distract and distract the eating experience. Clear the table of unnecessary items, creating a clean, inviting space for your meals.

Set the scene: Small touches like using an actual plate instead of eating out of a container, lighting a candle, or playing background music can enhance the mealtime atmosphere, making it easier to focus on eating. Invite company: Sharing a meal with others can be an excellent way to practice mindful eating. It encourages slower eating, engaging conversation, and a shared appreciation for the food and the moment. Integrating mindfulness into your eating habits means doing more than just nourishing your body. You're nourishing your mind and spirit, turning food into an ally in your quest for a more present, connected life. As you sit down to your next meal, remember that every bite is an opportunity to slow down, savor the moment, and reconnect with the simple yet profound act of eating.

3.4 Single-Tasking in a Multitasking World

In the digital age, we've glorified the art of juggling tasks like a circus performer with too many balls in the air. It's a badge of honor to be busy, to have dozens of tabs open on your computer, and to be in a perpetual state of doing multiple things at once. But here's the twist: multitasking isn't the hero we've made it out to be. It's often the villain in our story of stress and scattered focus.

The Myth of Multitasking

Let's get one thing straight: the human brain isn't wired to handle multiple tasks simultaneously efficiently. What we call multitasking is task-switching, a rapid shuffling back and forth between tasks. And every time you switch, there's a cost. Your brain needs a moment to catch up, leading to decreased productivity and increased mistakes. Not to mention, it feels like your mind's in a blender on high speed. Studies have shown that multitasking can reduce productivity by as much as

40%. It's a hard pill to swallow, but it's time to let go of the multitasking myth and embrace the untapped power of single-tasking.

The Benefits of Single-Tasking

Single-tasking is doing one thing at a time. It sounds deceptively simple, but its effects can be profound. By focusing on one task, you're giving it your full attention, which leads to:

Improved concentration: Without constantly switching gears, your brain can dive deep into the task.

Increased satisfaction: Completing a task from start to finish without interruption brings a sense of accomplishment that's hard to beat.

Enhanced performance: When you're not spreading yourself thin, the quality of your work improves. It's about doing fewer things better rather than more things worse.

Practical Single-Tasking Tips

So, how do you shift from multitasking to single-tasking? Here are some strategies to help you focus:

Prioritize your tasks: Only some things on your to-do list have equal weight. Identify the most critical task and tackle that first. Sometimes, it's about doing the right thing, not everything.

Set a timer: Allocate a specific amount of time to work on a task without interruption. You can use the Pomodoro Technique here or set a timer for 30-60 minutes and commit to focusing solely on your task during that time.

Limit distractions: Turn off notifications, close unnecessary tabs, and, if possible, find a quiet space where you can work undisturbed. This is about creating an environment that supports deep focus.

One tab rule: Challenge yourself to keep only one browser tab open at a time. It's a simple, effective way to ensure your digital environment is as clutter-free as your physical one.

Mindful Work Habits

Creating a workspace that encourages single-tasking and mindfulness is about more than just physical arrangements; it's a mindset. Here are some habits to cultivate:

Begin with intention: Before diving into a task, take a moment to set an intention. Ask yourself what you hope to achieve and how you want to approach the task. This helps align your actions with your goals.

Regular breaks: Paradoxically, stepping away from work can make you more productive. Regular breaks, especially ones that involve movement or a change of scenery, can refresh your mind and body, making it easier to maintain focus when you return to your task.

Clutter-free workspace: A cluttered desk can lead to a cluttered mind. Tidy your workspace for a few minutes at the start or end of each day. A clean, organized environment can significantly reduce stress and improve focus.

Mindful moments: Integrate short mindfulness exercises into your day. This could be a minute of deep breathing, a quick stretch, or a brief walk. These moments of mindfulness can help reset your focus and keep stress at bay.

In a world that celebrates the hustle and bustle of doing everything at once, choosing to single-task is a radical act of self-care. It's a commitment to showing up fully for each moment and task, valuing quality over quantity, and recognizing that sometimes, slowing down is the quickest way to get where you want to go. Mindfulness is one of the key tools in stopping burnout. As you read on, we will focus more and more on developing mindfulness across our lives and stopping burnout forever.

CHAPTER 4

SWEAT IT OUT, ZEN IT IN

"Exercise should be regarded as a tribute to the heart.

Gene Tunney

When I was advised to do physical exercise to help with stress, my first reaction was, "Are you joking? How am I going to fit that in?" It felt like another item on my to-do list, something else to try and squeeze in between all the other tasks. I was exhausted, and now I'm being told to go for a run and to wake up. Yet, somehow, it works. Exercise significantly contributes to beating stress, but how do you start?

4.1 Get Moving

The gym's excellent, with its shiny equipment and that unmistakable smell of determination (or is that disinfectant?). But there's a whole world of movement out there that can shake up your routine and keep the dreaded workout boredom at bay. Think outside the weights:

Dance like nobody's watching: Because sometimes, they aren't. Crank up your favorite tunes and let loose in your kitchen.

Take a hike: No, you don't need to scale Everest. A local trail or a walk in the park does wonders.

Bike to work: Swap the traffic jam for the bike lane. It's cardio with a view and eco-friendly to boot.

Join a sports league: It doesn't have to be hyper-competitive; it just needs fun. Local leagues offer everything from pickleball to frisbee, and it's a great way to meet people who want to avoid talking about work.

The psychological benefits of exercise

It's no secret that breaking a sweat is good for your body, but its impact on your mind is equally impressive. Regular physical activity can be a game-changer for your mood and mental health. It's like a natural antidepressant without the side effects. Exercise releases endorphins, those feel-good hormones that can lift your spirits and even dull pain. Plus, it's a proven stress-buster. Working out lowers cortisol levels, helping you feel more relaxed and less like a tightly wound spring.

Integrating movement into daily life

Carving out time for exercise can be a nightmare. The trick is to sneak movement into your day so seamlessly that it doesn't feel like a big deal. Stand-up meetings: Who said you have to sit? Propose standing or walking meetings. It's creativity and circulation in one.

Deskercise: Yes, it's a thing. Stretch, do chair squats, or even fidget. It all counts.

Park further away: Those distant parking spots? They're not just for latecomers. Treat it as a mini-walk to your destination.

Take the stairs: Elevators are great, but stairs are your mini-gym. Plus, no awkward elevator small talk.

Mindful exercise

Applying mindfulness to exercise means tuning into your body and the experience rather than zoning out or focusing solely on results. It's about feeling each movement, noticing your breath, and embracing the moment, whether it's a challenging climb on your bike or a serene stretch on your yoga mat.

Listen to your body: Pushing through pain isn't courage; it's a one-way ticket to injury. Respect your body's limits.

Focus on the now: Instead of obsessing over the calories burned or miles logged, pay attention to how your body feels in the moment–the rhythm of your breath, the strength in your muscles, the wind on your skin.

Savor the sensations: Exercise isn't just physical; it's a sensory experience. Notice the details–the texture of the ground beneath your feet, the sounds surrounding you, the patterns of your breath.

Blending mindfulness with movement transforms exercise from a mundane task into a rich, rewarding experience. It's no longer just about staying fit or blowing off steam; it's a practice in presence, a way to connect with yourself on a deeper level, and a path to finding peace in the pulse of everyday life.

So, there you have it. The journey from burnout doesn't require a passport or a pilgrimage to a mountaintop monastery. It's as simple as lacing up your sneakers, taking a deep breath, and stepping out the door. Remember whether sweating it out on the pavement or stretching it out on the mat. Every move you make is a step towards tranquility, a chance to weave a little more peace into the fabric of your daily life.

4.2 The Role of Nutrition in Managing Stress

Have you ever found yourself reaching for a snack when feeling on edge? It's not just you. Stress eating is a natural phenomenon. Unfortunately, while those sugary or salty treats might temporarily lift you, they're like loan sharks of the nutrition world. Sure, they'll lend you that quick hit of comfort, but the payback is a crash that leaves you feeling worse than before. Feeding your body the right stuff can be your secret weapon in the battle against stress.

Nutrition and Mental Health

Your brain is like a high-performance sports car. It performs best when it's appropriately fueled. Here's the deal: certain foods can relieve stress, while others can help keep you cruising smoothly. High-sugar snacks and ultra-processed foods can spike your blood sugar and then send it down, taking your mood and energy. On the flip side, a diet rich in whole foods provides steady fuel that helps buffer the effects of stress. It's about keeping the engine running smoothly without those disruptive stops and starts.

Foods that Fight Stress

Here's some help with what to pile on your plate to keep stress at bay: Omega-3 fatty acids: Think of these as your brain's best friends. In fatty fish like salmon, walnuts, and flaxseeds, omega-3s help keep the stress hormones cortisol and adrenaline from going haywire.

Leafy greens: Spinach, kale, and their relatives are loaded with magnesium, which is crucial in relaxing muscles and nerves. It's like a chill pill in food form.

Complex carbs: Oatmeal, whole grains, and sweet potatoes do more than keep you full. They help your brain produce serotonin, a neurotransmitter that's like a natural stress reliever.

Berries: These little powerhouses are packed with antioxidants, which help improve your body's response to stress and reduce inflammation. Probiotics: Foods like yogurt and kefir don't just keep your gut happy; they might also lower stress levels. Think of them as sending reinforcements to your body's natural stress-defense squad.

Incorporating these foods into your meals isn't about overhauling your diet overnight. It's more like making minor tweaks, one meal at a time. Swap out that white bread for whole grain, reach for a handful of almonds instead of a candy bar, or start your day with a bowl of oatmeal topped with berries. Small changes can lead to significant shifts in how you handle stress.

Mindful Eating Revisited

Here's where mindful eating circles back around. It's not just about what you eat; it's about how you eat. Tuning into your body's cues can help you distinguish between stress hunger and actual hunger. Before you reach for a snack, pause. Are you hungry, or are you trying to feed an emotion? This awareness can help you make better choices that serve your body and mind.

Check-in with yourself: Take a moment to assess your hunger. Is it your stomach asking for food, boredom, or stress knocking at the door?

Eat without distractions: Sitting down without the TV or phone can help you focus on your food and how it makes you feel.

Savor the flavor: Slow down and taste your food. This can help you enjoy it more and feel satisfied with less.

Hydration and Stress

Last but certainly not least, let's talk about water. It's easy to overlook, but staying hydrated reduces stress levels. Even mild dehydration can affect your mood and energy, making managing stress more challenging. Aim to keep a bottle of water nearby and sip throughout the day. If you find plain water boring, jazz it up with a squeeze of lemon, a mint sprig, or a cucumber slice.

Water's role extends beyond just quenching thirst. It helps your brain function at its best, keeps your energy up, and even reduces the likelihood of stress-induced headaches. So, the next time you feel wound up, reach for a glass of water. It is the most straightforward, most effective stress-reduction tool in your arsenal.

Navigating the waters of stress management requires more than just a good night's sleep or a jog around the block. What you put on your plate plays a starring role in how you feel physically and mentally. By choosing foods that fuel your body and brain, practicing mindful eating, and keeping hydration in check, you're setting yourself up for success. It's about creating a foundation that supports you through life's ups and downs, keeping you resilient, focused, and ready to face whatever comes your way with a sense of calm and clarity.

4.3 Sleep Hygiene for Better Rest and Recovery

Tossing and turning through the night, counting sheep, or staring at the ceiling doesn't just rob you of rest; it sets you up for a day fueled by caffeine and short-fused responses. It's a vicious cycle, with stress bulldozing your sleep and the lack of it piling on more stress. But here's the good news: breaking this cycle is easier. A few tweaks to your nighttime routine and sleep environment can smooth the path to good rest, making those eight hours of shut-eye less of a myth and more of a nightly reality.

The Tug of War Between Sleep and Stress

It's like they're pulling with all their might at opposite ends of a rope. Stress cranks your body's alertness, flooding your system with adrenaline and cortisol, making relaxation a tall order. On the flip side, skimping on sleep leaves your body in a state of high alert, sensitive to stressors you'd usually shrug off. Step one is recognizing this link; step two is taking action to ensure your body isn't primed for a fight when your head hits the pillow

4.4 Mindfulness Before Bed: Ending the Day on a Positive Note

A mindful evening routine is like giving yourself a high-five for making it through another 24 hours. It's your chance to wash off the day's grime–literally and figuratively–and prep for a night of restorative sleep. This wind-down period is your cue to the mind and body that the hustle is over and it's time to switch gears.

The Importance of a Wind-Down Routine

Why bother with a nighttime routine? Think of it as laying the groundwork for quality sleep. It's your body's version of closing down tabs before shutting off the computer. A consistent routine helps signal that sleep is on the horizon, making it easier to drift off and stay asleep. Plus, it's your chance to shake off any stress or tension, so you're not taking it to bed.

Mindful Reflection

Reflecting on your day can be as calming as a cup of chamomile tea. The trick is to do it without judgment. Instead of replaying mistakes or fretting over what you didn't get done, focus on the wins, no matter how small. Did you remember to drink water? Score. Held the door for a stranger? Great. This isn't about tallying achievements but acknowledging the day's efforts and learning moments.

Here's how to weave mindful reflection into your evening:

Keep a gratitude journal: Jot down three things you're grateful for daily. It could be anything from a delicious meal to a warm shower.

Reflect on interactions: Think about the conversations and interactions you had. What went well? What could you improve? How did they make you feel?

Ponder one thing you learned: Aim to learn something new every day, no matter how trivial it may seem.

Relaxation Techniques

Your body needs to be on the same page as your mind regarding winding down. Here are a couple of relaxation techniques to ease into sleep:

Progressive muscle relaxation: Starting at your toes and working up to your head, tense each muscle group for a few seconds, then release. It helps release physical tension and signals your body to rest.

Guided imagery: Visualize a peaceful scene, a place that feels safe and relaxed. Engage all your senses to make it as vivid as possible. This technique is like a mini-vacation for your brain, steering it towards tranquility.

Crafting a Pre-Sleep Ritual

Think of this as setting the stage for an excellent performance. Your evening routine can signal your body that it's time to wind down. Here's how to craft yours:

Dim the lights: Bright light tricks your brain into thinking it's still go-time. As evening falls, opt for softer, warmer lighting to coax your body into relaxation mode.

Ease up on electronics: Phones, tablets, and laptops are double trouble, emitting sleep-disruptive blue light and often stressing content. Aim to switch off at least an hour before bed. If you must use them, consider a blue light filter.

Warm bath or shower: The drop in body temperature after a warm bath or shower can signal your body it's time to sleep, mimicking the natural drop in your internal thermostat that occurs at night.

Relaxation exercises: Gentle stretching, deep breathing, or progressive muscle relaxation can help release physical tension and quiet a busy mind.

Crafting Your Dream Sleep Haven

Creating a sanctuary for quality sleep begins with transforming your bedroom into a haven of tranquility. Here are some essential steps to elevate your sleep environment:

Maintain the Perfect Temperature: Did you know the ideal temperature for optimal sleep is 60-67 degrees Fahrenheit? This range mimics your body's natural nighttime drop in temperature, promoting deeper and more restful sleep. Consider adjusting your thermostat or investing in bedding materials that help regulate temperature to achieve this sleep-inducing ambiance.

Embrace the Darkness: Light can disrupt your sleep patterns and hinder your ability to fall and stay asleep. Combat this by investing in blackout curtains or a cozy sleep mask to block out unwanted light sources such as streetlights or early morning sunbeams. By creating a dark environment, you signal to your brain that it's time to wind down and prepare for restorative sleep.

Silence is Golden: External noises can be a significant sleep disruptor, leading to frequent awakenings or difficulty falling asleep. If you cannot control ambient noise levels, consider incorporating white noise machines or using earplugs to create a calm and consistent auditory environment conducive to sleep. By minimizing disruptive sounds, you can enjoy uninterrupted rest throughout the night.

Prioritize Comfort: The foundation of a rejuvenating sleep experience lies in investing in quality bedding essentials. Opt for a supportive mattress and pillows that cater to your unique sleeping position and comfort preferences. Whether you prefer plush softness or firm support, selecting the right bedding ensures you look forward to slipping into bed each night, embracing a cocoon of comfort and relaxation.

By implementing these strategies, you can transform your bedroom into a sanctuary dedicated to promoting restful and rejuvenating sleep. This will ensure you awaken each morning feeling refreshed and ready to embrace the day ahead.

Navigating the Night's Obstacles

Even with the best intentions, sometimes sleep plays hard to get, and you find yourself wide awake at 3 a.m. Here's how to handle common sleep disturbances:

If you can't fall asleep, Don't force it. Lying in bed wide awake can lead to frustration. Get up, do something low-key like reading or listening to soothing music in dim light, then try again once you feel sleepier.

Waking up in the night: Stay calm. Avoid looking at the clock, as it can increase stress about how little you're sleeping. Deep breathing or visualization can help lull you back to sleep.

Consistent wake-up time: Even on weekends, try to get up around the same time. It helps anchor your body's internal clock, making it easier to fall asleep and wake up naturally.

In the dance between stress and sleep, leading with intention and some strategy can tip the scales in your favor. By setting the right scene for sleep in your routine and environment and learning how to sidestep potential pitfalls during the night, you're not just investing in better rest but paving the way for calmer, more peace-filled days.

By carving out time each evening for these practices, you're setting the stage for a good night's sleep and cultivating a sense of calm and mindfulness beyond the bedroom. It's a way of bookending your day with intention, a reminder that you can create moments of peace and reflection despite the chaos and noise.

And just like that, the day comes to a close. You've navigated the twists and turns from opening your eyes to the last flicker of consciousness before sleep. Each practice, from your morning rituals to your evening wind-down, isn't just about that moment; it's a thread in the larger tapestry of living mindfully. As you drift off, know that you're weaving a life where peace isn't just a visitor but a familiar friend. Tomorrow is another day, another opportunity to live fully and breathe deeply.

4.5 Breathing Techniques for Instant Calm

You know those moments when the world is spinning at a million miles per hour, and you're clinging on for dear life? Let's talk about hitting the brakes, not with a screeching halt, but with something as simple and profound as your breath. It's the unsung hero in your body's toolkit, a direct hotline to dialing down stress and tuning into calm. So, how does this magic work? Let's dive in.

The Science of Breath and Stress

When stress has you in its grips, your body doesn't know if you're facing a grizzly bear or a mountain of emails. It just reacts, launching into fight-or-flight mode. Here's where controlled breathing comes in. By taking slow, deliberate breaths, you're sending your brain a signal saying, "Hey, it's cool. We got this." This activates your parasympathetic nervous system, the chill counterpart to stress's alarm bells. The result? Your heart rate slows, muscles relax, and your mind realizes the crisis is averted or manageable.

Breathing Exercises for Stress Management

Ready to harness the power of your breath? Here are a couple of techniques to get you started:

Belly Breathing: Place one hand on your chest and the other on your belly. Inhale deeply through your nose, aiming to raise the hand on your belly more than the one on your chest. Exhale slowly. This will get more oxygen into your system, which can be a game-changer for stress levels. Alternate Nostril Breathing: This one might sound out there, but stick with me. Close off one nostril with a finger, inhale through the open one, close it off, then exhale through the other nostril. It's a rhythmic way to balance your mind and body.

Integrating Breathing Exercises into Daily Life

When is the prime time to practice these breathing techniques? Here are a few suggestions:

Before the morning rush: Take a few minutes to center yourself with deep breaths when you wake up. It sets a calm tone for whatever the day throws at you.

In the heat of the moment: Feel yourself getting riled up in a meeting or stuck in traffic? That's your cue. A minute of focused breathing can be your invisible shield against stress.

Pre-sleep wind-down: Help your body transition to sleep mode with gentle breathing exercises. It's like telling your brain, "Time to power down."

Making Breathing Exercises a Habit

Consistency is key. To make these breathing exercises stick, try:
Setting reminders: Set a few reminders on your phone or computer. For example, a prompt that says, "Breathe," can be enough to get you into the habit.

Tie it to daily tasks: Link your breathing practice to something you do regularly, like boiling the kettle or waiting for your computer to boot up. This will help you build a natural rhythm for the practice throughout the day.

Patience and persistence: Some days, it'll feel like second nature. Others, not so much. Keep at it. The benefits to your stress levels and overall well-being are worth the effort.

And there you have it. Breathing is fundamental yet incredibly powerful and can be your secret weapon against stress. It's not about adding another task to your overloaded list. It's about giving yourself a moment to step back, recalibrate, and approach life's challenges with a more precise, calmer mind.

Remember: amidst the hustle and bustle of daily life, your breath remains a constant, a rope keeping you anchored in the present. With each inhale and exhale, you can pause, reset, and move forward with peace and presence. It's a simple yet profound practice that holds the key to navigating the ebb and flow of life's stresses with grace and resilience. In the next chapter, we'll explore more tools and techniques to build your oasis of calm amid life's storms.

Nobody on their death bed has ever said,

CHAPTER 5
PROFESSIONAL BURNOUT

"I wish I had spent more time at the office."
Rabbi Harold Kushner

Burnout is most apparent in our professional lives. This chapter will examine how we incorporate mindfulness into our work and how doing so can stave off burnout.

5.1 Understanding Imposter Syndrome

Ever felt like you're doing a tightrope walk in your professional life, balancing so precariously that one misstep could send you plummeting? You're constantly proving yourself, battling the nagging doubt you don't quite measure up. Welcome to Club Imposter Syndrome.

Imposter Syndrome isn't just about feeling out of your depth; it's a full-blown script in your head that constantly whispers, "You're a fraud, and soon, everyone's going to find out." Sound familiar? You're not alone. It's like you've got an annoying roommate in your head, critiquing your every move. Recognizing this unwelcome guest is the first step in serving it an eviction notice.

Now, we are going to talk about affirmations.

If you're anything like me, when you hear the term 'affirmations, ' you roll your eyes and shake your head. However, it turns out affirmations work–not the fluffy "I am a unicorn" kind, but genuine affirmations tailored to you.

They can start as simply as:

"I'm doing my best in every situation."

"I've got the skills required."

"I believe in my ability to conquer challenges."

These short declarations are more than just positive self-talk; they're your mental toolkit for redirecting focus away from perceived shortcomings toward your existing strengths and those you're eager to develop.

But do affirmations indeed wield magic? Well, not exactly.

Affirmations act as a mind-shifting tool to propel you toward your goals. Still, they won't miraculously fast-track your success or instantly heal wounds.

How they work

Enter neuroplasticity, your brain's adaptive prowess. It's the key to understanding why affirmations work and how to supercharge their impact. Your brain occasionally blurs the lines between imagination and reality. This phenomenon can be surprisingly advantageous.

Visualize yourself acing that nerve-wracking interview or conquering your fear of heights through bungee jumping. Remarkably, the same brain regions light up as you live in these scenarios. Consistently affirming positive statements nudges your brain to treat them as undeniable truths. When you genuinely believe in your capabilities, your actions are often quick to follow suit.

Consider swapping out a negative thought like:

"I'm terrible at interviews. I'm less qualified than others. They won't hire me; I should leave."

With a positive affirmation:

"I possess all the skills and experience needed. I am the perfect fit for this job."

Affirmations can ease pre-interview jitters, and the assurance of readiness can shield you from self-sabotaging thoughts that might hinder your success.

Remember, action is paramount.

Repeating affirmations boosts motivation and confidence, but the key lies in your actions. Affirmations are a stepping stone to change, not the change itself.

Think about that nosy co-worker prying into your personal life. An affirmation like "I can remain calm even when annoyed" might guide

How to Stop Burnout

you to deep breathing or grounding exercises, maintaining composure until you can gracefully exit the conversation.

The affirmation didn't make the change; you did. It merely paved the way.

Enhancing their effectiveness

Affirmations are just one tool in the self-help kit. Their impact depends on how you wield them. Craft your affirmations to ensure they align with your goals. Consider these tips to boost their effectiveness:

Set them in the present: Affirmations aren't goals. They're about changing ingrained patterns and beliefs. While a goal is something to work towards, an affirmation reinforces your confidence in what you can do now.

Avoid stock affirmations: You can find affirmations everywhere, but tailoring them to your goals is critical. Get creative, link them to your core values, and make them as specific as possible. For instance: "I have wonderful co-workers and a loving family. My work satisfies me, and I know I'm making a difference."

Keep it accurate: Affirmations work best when focusing on specific traits or realistic, achievable changes. Acknowledge that some changes are easier than others. For example: "I appreciate what my body does for me each day, and I keep myself in good health with regular activity and nutritious foods."

Practice daily: For maximum benefit, establish a routine. Dedicate 3 to 5 minutes twice daily to repeat each affirmation ten times. Believe in their truth as you utter them. If possible, involve a trusted loved one to reinforce your belief.

Be patient. Changes may take time, so commit to your practice.

5.2 Dealing with Difficult Colleagues

In your workplace's bustling drama, you're bound to bump into a few colleagues who don't make your job sweeter. Whether it's the overbearing project manager or the cubicle mate who won't use headphones, navigating these choppy waters requires a blend of tact and patience.

Pinpointing the Trouble Spots

First, let's figure out why you are irritated by this person. Is it a clash of work styles where your meticulous planning hits a wall against their fly-by-the-seat-of-their-pants approach? Or the other way around? It may be an issue that's come up because communication has hit a snag. You know how it is with emails – they're super handy but not exactly great at capturing the subtleties and feelings behind our words. So, what happens? Well, messages sent through email can easily get lost in translation, leading to conflicts or misunderstandings. Recognizing the roots can turn an abstract annoyance into a problem you can tackle.

I used to work in a large open-plan office with about fifty colleagues. One person who sat two desks behind me insisted on emailing me problems instead of taking 10 seconds to walk over and talk to me. It used to drive me mad, and I didn't handle it well. I thought they were rude and arrogant, and we fought nonstop. Looking back with the benefit of hindsight, it was a clash over working styles.

Work styles: Everyone's got their rhythm. Identifying where these rhythms clash can help in finding a middle ground.

Communication habits: Misunderstandings often stem from mismatched communication styles. Are they a talker while you're a texter?

Personal vs. professional: Sometimes, personal quirks seep into professional spaces. Pinpoint if the conflict is work-related or if personal annoyances are at play.

Mindfulness as Your Secret Weapon

We can use mindfulness to diffuse tension. Here's how:
Pause before reacting: Feel that knee-jerk reaction coming on? Hit the pause button. A breath or two can change the game, giving you space to respond rather than react.

Observe without judgment: Try to see the situation from a birds-eye view without labeling it right or wrong. It's not about excusing behavior but about understanding it.

Respond with calm: Once you've mastered your emotions, address the issue directly but gently. A calm demeanor can often disarm tension.

Empathy: The Bridge Over Troubled Water

Empathy, in this context, doesn't mean agreeing with or condoning someone's actions. It's about understanding their perspective, which can be a powerful tool in resolving conflicts. Here's how to cultivate it: Ask, don't assume: Got a bone to pick? Ask them about their perspective first. You might find the intentions behind their actions are far from what you imagined.

Find common ground: Often, you're both aiming for the same goal–the project or team's success. Highlighting shared objectives can realign conflicting paths.

Offer support: Sometimes, challenging behavior stems from feeling overwhelmed or underappreciated. A simple "How can I help?" can work wonders.

Setting Boundaries with Professional Polish

Last but not least, remember what we learned about boundaries. They're not walls but lines in the sand that protect your peace and productivity. Here's how to set them like a pro:

Be clear and direct: Wishy-washy boundaries serve no one. Be specific about what is and isn't acceptable in your professional interaction.

Consistency is key: Once you've set a boundary, stick to it. Consistency reinforces your expectations.

Offer alternatives: If you're saying no to one thing, try to offer another solution. "I can't stay late tonight, but I'm free to tackle this first thing in the morning."

In office dynamics, dealing with difficult colleagues doesn't have to be all stress and frustration. With insight into the sources of conflict, the calming influence of mindfulness, the bridge-building power of empathy, and the clear lines drawn by effective boundaries, you can build a more harmonious workspace. Remember, it's not about changing others but adjusting your responses and approaches to foster a more positive, productive, professional environment.

5.3 Setting Realistic Goals and Celebrating Small Wins

In the hustle of our professional lives, it's easy to get caught up in the chase for the next significant achievement, the vast win that'll make everything fall into place. But here's a thought: what if the real game-changer lies in setting goals that don't stretch you so thin that you're practically see-through? What if the answer to professional satisfaction and reducing burnout is setting realistic goals, acknowledging the small victories, and tracking your progress with a kind eye? Let's break this down and see how this can transform goal setting from a stress-inducing race to a fulfilling, mindful journey.

Mindful Goal-Setting

The mindfulness approach to setting goals flips the script on traditional goal-setting. Instead of aiming for the stars with a cannon, it's about stepping back and aligning your goals with your deepest values and professional aspirations. It's asking not just "What do I want to achieve?" but "Why do I want to achieve this, and how does it reflect who I am and what I believe in?" This alignment ensures that your goals are not just achievable but meaningful. Here's how to get started:

Break it down: Start with the big picture and break it into smaller, manageable goals. This makes the journey feel less daunting and more doable.

Be specific: Vague goals are the enemy of progress. "Become a better presenter" is a noble aim, but "Attend one public speaking workshop by next month" gives you a clear target and timeframe.

Flexibility is your friend: Remember, goals are not set in stone. Life throws curveballs, and being able to adjust your goals keeps you moving forward without beating yourself up over unforeseen changes.

The Importance of Celebrating Progress

Now, for the fun part: celebrating your wins. In the relentless pursuit of success, it's easy to overlook the milestones you've crossed and your progress. But acknowledging and celebrating these achievements, no matter how small, is a powerful motivator. It's a reminder that you're moving in the right direction and that your efforts bear fruit.

I used to make my team stop and celebrate whenever they achieved something. I would ask them if they had drank champagne and danced on the tables to celebrate. More often than not, they would be rushing on to the next project, claiming they needed more time to pause. But that diminishes their accomplishments, robs them of the joy of achievement, and leads them towards burnout.

So, how do you make a habit of this?

Keep a win journal: Jot down your achievements, big and small. Flipping through the journal on a rough day can be a considerable boost and remind you why you do what you do.

Share your successes: Whether it's with a mentor, colleague, or friend, sharing your wins not only validates your efforts but can also inspire others.

Reward yourself: Have you finished a challenging project? Treat yourself to something you enjoy, be it a fancy coffee or a movie night. Or if you are in the mood, why not drink champagne and dance on the tables?

Mindful Tracking of Progress

Tracking your progress toward your goals is essential, but the "how" makes all the difference. Instead of obsessively ticking off boxes and berating yourself for any perceived lack of progress, adopt a mindful approach. This means observing your progress without judgment, acknowledging the efforts you've put in, and understanding that every step, no matter how small, is part of your growth. Consider these methods:

Set regular check-ins: Schedule times to review your goals and progress. This isn't about self-critique but about self-reflection and adjustment.

Use visual aids: Charts, graphs, or even a simple list on your wall can give you a tangible sense of your journey and accomplishments.

Celebrate the learning: Every goal, achieved or not, comes with its lessons. Recognizing what you've learned is as vital as celebrating your accomplishments.

Adjusting Goals with Flexibility

Flexibility in goal setting is not about giving yourself an out whenever things get tough; it's about recognizing that both you and your circumstances evolve. A goal made perfect sense six months ago might not align with your current reality or aspirations. Being flexible allows you to recalibrate your goals to fit your growth and the shifts in your professional landscape. Here's how to stay adaptable:

Periodic reassessment: Every once in a while, take a step back and assess your goals. Do they still align with your aspirations and values?

Embrace the detours: Sometimes, the path to your goal takes unexpected turns. Instead of resisting, look for the opportunities these detours might offer.

Adjust and communicate: When adjusting your goals, ensure you communicate these changes to any relevant parties, be it your team, your mentor, or your boss. This keeps everyone on the same page and supports your journey.

Incorporating mindfulness into your goal-setting and achievement strategy transforms what could be a source of stress into a more balanced, fulfilling pursuit. It's about setting goals that resonate with your core, celebrating the steps you take, tracking your journey with a gentle gaze, and remaining fluid as you grow and evolve. This approach bolsters your professional development and enriches your personal growth, making each step forward a testament to your resilience, dedication, and mindfulness.

5.4 Mindful Communication in Professional Settings

In the bustling arenas of our work lives, where emails fly faster than light, and meetings stack up like Tetris blocks, the art of communication often gets lost in translation. Mindful communication isn't about quoting the Eastern philosophy of Marcus Aurelius's *Meditations*; it's about ensuring that when you speak or listen, it's with purpose, presence, and, most importantly, a human touch. It's about turning every interaction from a potential minefield into an opportunity for connection and understanding.

The Core of Mindful Communication

At its heart, mindful communication involves two key players: the speaker and the listener. For the speaker, it means sharing thoughts in a way that's clear, concise, and considerate of the listener's perspective. For the listener, it's about tuning in with full attention, free from the usual distractions that tug at our minds. Here's how you can bring this into play:

When speaking, pause first. Reflect on what you want to convey and why it matters. This helps you trim the fat and get to the meat of your message.

Make eye contact as a listener. It's a nonverbal nod that says, "I'm here, and I'm with you." It makes a world of difference.

Keep distractions at bay. Close that laptop, silence your phone, and give the conversation the space it deserves.

Steering Through Tough Talks

Ah, difficult conversations - the broccoli of the professional diet. We know they're good for us, resolving issues and clearing the air, but that doesn't make them any easier to digest. Here's where mindfulness can be a lifesaver, turning these chats from dreaded ordeals into constructive dialogues:

Start with empathy. Try to understand where the other person is coming from, even if you disagree. It's like putting on their shoes for a quick walk around the block - uncomfortable, yes, but enlightening.

Use "I" statements. Instead of saying, "You always miss deadlines," try, "I feel concerned when deadlines are missed." This shifts the focus from blame to impact, making it easier for the other party to hear you out without going on the defensive.

Breathe. Yes, it sounds too simple, but a deep breath can be the pause button to collect your thoughts and prevent the conversation from overheating.

Fueling Team Synergy

Something magical happens when mindful communication becomes the norm rather than the exception within a team. Collaboration doesn't just improve; it flourishes. Ideas bounce back and forth quickly, solutions emerge from the collective brainstorming, and the team moves as one cohesive unit. Here are some strategies to foster this environment:

Encourage open forums. Regular meetings where team members can voice ideas and concerns without fear of judgment create a culture of openness and trust.

Celebrate the diversity of thought. Remind your team that different perspectives aren't just welcome but invaluable. It's the spice blend that makes the final dish delightful.

Practice active listening as a group. During discussions, have team members summarize the speaker's point before adding their thoughts. It ensures everyone is heard and understood.

Cultivating Gratitude in Every Exchange

Imagine ending a workday feeling appreciated and seen - not for a significant win, but for your everyday efforts. This is the power of weaving gratitude into your communication. It's a simple yet profound shift that can transform workplace dynamics:

Say, thank you. A genuine thank you goes a long way, whether you're thanking a colleague for staying late to help with a project or someone for simply refilling the coffee maker.

Give kudos. Public acknowledgments during meetings for both big and small contributions spotlight the value each team member brings and foster a culture of appreciation.
Personalize your appreciation. A handwritten note, a quick message,

or a small gesture tailored to the person you're thanking makes the expression of gratitude more sincere and impactful.

In the tapestry of professional interactions, threads of mindful communication weave patterns of clarity, empathy, and respect. It's about more than just exchanging information; it's about connecting, understanding, and building relationships that stand the test of workplace pressures. Through mindful speaking and listening, navigating difficult conversations with grace, fostering team collaboration, and infusing every interaction with gratitude, we don't just communicate; we connect on a level that transcends the transactional nature of work, creating an environment where everyone feels valued, heard, and motivated to contribute their best.

5.5 Mindfulness in Leadership and Teamwork

In the bustling workplace ecosystem, where different personalities and ambitions often collide, a leader's role is guiding, inspiring, and maintaining harmony. It's a delicate dance that requires strategic insight and a profound understanding of human nature and the principles of mindfulness. Here, we explore how the essence of mindfulness can transform leadership and teamwork, creating an environment where growth, respect, and adaptability flourish.

Leading with Mindfulness

Mindful leadership is about presence. It's about showing up fully for your team physically, mentally, and emotionally. This approach fosters a work culture where people feel seen, heard, and valued, setting the stage for genuine engagement and collaboration. Here are some ways to embody this leadership style:

Walk the talk: Your actions speak volumes. When you embody the values you preach, you set a powerful example for your team.

Foster a positive environment: Recognize achievements, provide constructive feedback, and cultivate a workspace where mistakes are seen as learning opportunities.

Promote well-being: Encourage breaks, support work-life balance, and create channels for open communication about stress and workload.

Building Cohesive Teams with Mindfulness

Let's talk about mindfulness in the area of teamwork. Picture this: a group of diverse individuals coming together to work and thrive. How do you make that happen? It's not easy, but here are a few strategies to help you on the way:

Embrace Diversity: Consider your team a melting pot of talents and quirks. Celebrate the unique strengths each person brings to the table. After all, it's this mix of skills, perspectives, and approaches that spices up collaboration and sparks creativity.

Keep it Respectful: Imagine a place where every idea is welcome, decisions are made as a team, and disagreements are handled empathetically. That's the kind of atmosphere you want to cultivate. Respect is the essential ingredient that keeps the team humming along smoothly.

Get on the Same Page: It is crucial to know what needs to get done and how to do it. But understanding why you're doing it together can make all the difference. So, take a moment to align on your shared goals. Knowing the 'why' behind your team's mission adds a dash of purpose to your collective efforts, making them feel less like work and more like a meaningful journey.

Encouraging Personal and Professional Growth

A key aspect of mindful leadership is supporting the holistic development of team members. It's about identifying and nurturing their potential, encouraging them to meet and exceed their expectations. Here's how you can be a catalyst for their growth:

Individualized development plans: Work with each team member to set personalized goals that align with their aspirations and the team's needs.

Continuous learning opportunities: Foster an environment where learning is ongoing, whether through formal training, mentoring, or cross-functional projects.

Feedback and reflection: Regular, meaningful feedback helps individuals recognize their progress, understand areas for improvement, and reflect on their journey.

Navigating Change with Grace

Change is the only constant in the business world, and leading a team through it requires a laser focus on adaptability and calmness. When change looms, how you steer your team can spark innovation and resilience or lead to resistance and fear. Here are a few pointers for navigating these waters smoothly:

Communicate openly and often: Keep the lines of communication open and provide clear, honest information about the change and how it impacts the team.

Involve the team in the process: Give team members a voice in implementing the change. This fosters a sense of ownership and can ease the transition.

Maintain a steady presence: Your team looks to you for reaction cues. Staying calm, collected, and optimistic sets a positive tone, even in uncertainty.

When we weave mindfulness into how we lead and work together, we have a powerful tool for tackling burnout head-on. It's all about focusing on connection, compassion, and sharing the journey toward success. This makes our work environment richer and spills over into our personal lives, fostering a vibe of respect, growth, and resilience for everyone involved. And as we wrap up this chat about using mindfulness to beat burnout at work, let's remember the real essence of what we're doing here. It's not about chasing after individual awards; it's about the journey we're all on together, aiming for meaning, fulfillment, and excellence. Let's keep building spaces where everyone can shine, tackle challenges gracefully, and celebrate each win as a team victory.

CHAPTER 6

MINDFUL CONNECTIONS:

"Friendship is the hardest thing in the world to explain.
It's not something you learn in school.
But if you haven't learned the meaning of friendship,
you really haven't learned anything."

Muhammad Ali

The famous poem says, "No man is an island; no man lives alone." Unfortunately, in our modern world, that is too often the case. A 2021 study showed that only about 1 in 5 men had received emotional support from a friend in the last week. It is marginally better for Women, with 2 in 5 saying they received support. This chapter is aimed at helping you develop mindful connections. The kind of relationship that helps you when you're burnt out and can prevent you from getting there in the first place.

6.1 Vulnerability as Strength

There's a common myth that vulnerability equals weakness, a sign that you're not cut out for the rough and tumble of real life. That's idiotic and dangerous. Allowing yourself to be vulnerable is one of the bravest things you can do. It's the cornerstone of deep, authentic connections. Just like a seed needs to break open to sprout, opening up in relationships can lead to growth you never imagined.

Re-imagining vulnerability: It's about seeing vulnerability not as opening the door to judgment or pity but as an invitation for genuine connection.

Real-life example: Consider when a friend shared something personal with you. Chances are, it didn't make you think less of them. More likely, it brought you closer. That's vulnerability in action.

Practicing Vulnerability Mindfully

Opening up shouldn't be like a floodgate opening–everything pouring out simultaneously. It's more about a gradual unveiling, a mindful sharing that fosters closeness and trust. Here's how to approach it:
Start small: Sharing doesn't have to be about revealing your deepest,

darkest secrets. It can be as simple as expressing your feelings about a movie you watched together.

Choose the right moment: Timing matters. There might be better settings than a crowded party for sharing personal thoughts. Look for quiet, intimate moments.

Be honest but considerate: It's about sharing your truth without offloading every single worry or fear. Think of it as offering a window into your world, not throwing open the doors to a hurricane.

Setting Boundaries for Safe Vulnerability

Boundaries and vulnerability might seem like opposites, but they're two sides of the same coin. Boundaries help create a safe space for vulnerability, a framework within which you can open up without feeling exposed or overwhelmed.

Know your limits: Understanding your comfort levels is critical. It's okay to say, "This is something I'm not ready to talk about yet."

Communicate your boundaries: Let the other person know where your line is. It's not about shutting down the conversation but guiding it where you both feel comfortable.

Respect their boundaries: Just as you have limits, so do they. Pay attention to verbal and non-verbal cues that might indicate they're uncomfortable.

The Impact of Vulnerability on Relationships

When both people in a relationship embrace vulnerability, it can lead to transformations that are nothing short of remarkable. It's like nurturing a plant with just enough water and sunlight.

Deepened trust: Sharing personal thoughts and feelings can build a foundation of rock-solid trust, making the relationship more robust and resilient.

Enhanced communication: Vulnerability opens up new communication channels, making it easier to talk about everything from the day-to-day stuff to the big, life-changing decisions.

Greater intimacy: There's an intimacy that comes from truly knowing someone, warts and all. It's a closeness that goes beyond the physical, rooted in emotional and mental connection.

Imagine a chart plotting the relationship between vulnerability and connection for a visual element. You have a vulnerability on one axis, from 'Surface Level' to 'Deep Sharing.' On the other hand, there is a connection between 'Acquaintance' and 'Deep bond.' As vulnerability increases, so does the depth of the connection.

Mindful vulnerability can lead you to connections that are not just fulfilling but transformative. It's about opening up, setting boundaries to keep that openness safe, and watching your relationships grow more profound and meaningful. Just remember, vulnerability is a two-way street—it's as much about listening and holding space for others as it is about sharing your thoughts and feelings. So, take that step, share a little, and watch your connections blossom into something extraordinary.

6.2 Active Listening: A Path to Deeper Relationships

Listening isn't just about letting sound waves hit your eardrums. It's about tuning in, catching every word, and understanding the music behind the lyrics—the emotions, the unspoken thoughts, the subtle invitations to dive deeper into someone's world. This is the essence of active listening, a skill that transforms everyday chit-chat into meaningful dialogue, strengthening the bonds we share with others.

Listening with Intent

Active listening is a galaxy away from its distant cousin, passive hearing. The latter is when you hear words but don't absorb them. Your mind might wander, thinking about what to have for dinner or that email you forgot to send. On the other hand, active listening is when you're fully present, giving your undivided attention to the speaker. It's listening to truly understand the other person's perspective without immediately thinking about how to respond or what advice to give.

The Role of Mindfulness in Active Listening

Mindfulness is the secret that takes active listening from good to great.

It involves being entirely in the moment, brushing away distractions like a chef flicks flour from their apron. Here's how to sprinkle some mindfulness into your listening:

Focus on the now: Let go of thoughts about the past or the future. If your mind drifts, gently nudge it back to the conversation.

Notice body language: Sometimes, what isn't said speaks volumes. Pay attention to facial expressions, gestures, and posture–like subtitles to the spoken words.

Embrace silence: Don't rush to fill pauses with your own words. Silence can be a space for the speaker to gather thoughts or for deeper insights to bubble up.

Practicing Active Listening in Everyday Interactions

Turning active listening into a habit doesn't require a Herculean effort. It's about making minor adjustments in how you engage with others. Here are a few exercises to help you get there:

Repeat back: After someone shares something with you, paraphrase what they've said to confirm your understanding. It shows you're paying attention and clarifies any miscommunications.

Ask open-ended questions: These are questions that can't be answered with a simple "yes" or "no." They encourage the speaker to open up and share more, showing you're interested in digging deeper.

Be patient: Resist the urge to jump in with solutions or opinions. Sometimes, people need to be heard, not fixed.

Overcoming Barriers to Active Listening

Even with the best intentions, a few roadblocks can challenge active listening. Recognizing and navigating these obstacles is part of the journey:

Distractions: Our brains are like browsers with too many tabs open. To minimize distractions, find a quiet spot for conversations when possible, put away devices, and give the speaker your full visual attention.

Judgment: Forming opinions before the other person finishes speaking is easy. Make a conscious effort to keep an open mind, setting aside your biases and judgments.

Waiting to speak: Sometimes, we're so focused on what we want to say next that we must fully listen. Challenge yourself to let go of this urge. Your response will be more thoughtful and relevant if it's informed by truly listening first.

By weaving active listening into the fabric of your interactions, you are hearing more and understanding better. It's a skill that enriches your relationships, making every conversation an opportunity to connect on a deeper level. Whether with a partner, friend, or colleague, active listening is a testament to your respect and care for the person before you, a step towards more meaningful, fulfilling connections.

6.3 Setting Boundaries in Personal Life

You're at a bustling family gathering, everyone's having a grand time, and Uncle Joe corners you to grill you about when you're getting a "real job," marrying, or having kids. You laugh it off, but inside, you want to tell him to take a walk. It's a classic case of personal boundaries being trampled on, and moments like these highlight the critical role boundaries play in maintaining our well-being and the health of our relationships.

The Foundation of Healthy Relationships

Boundaries are the threads that maintain the tapestry of human connections' strength and integrity. They're not walls meant to keep people out but guidelines that help us respect each other's personal space, values, and needs. These guidelines are necessary for relationships to become breeding grounds for resentment, misunderstanding, and conflict.

Preventing resentment: Clear boundaries help ensure you don't overextend yourself, safeguarding against bitterness from being taken advantage of.

Fostering mutual respect: When both parties understand and respect each other's boundaries, a foundation of respect strengthens the relationship.

Encouraging independence: Healthy boundaries allow for individual growth and freedom within the relationship, preventing co-dependency.

Identifying Your Boundaries

Recognizing your boundaries starts with some introspection. Consider what makes you feel comfortable, respected, and valued. Reflect on past interactions that left you feeling the opposite–those moments often point directly to a crossed boundary.

Physical boundaries relate to your need for personal space or discomfort with certain types of physical contact.

Emotional boundaries: Consider what emotional behaviors you're okay with. How much of your own and others' emotional burdens can you handle?

Time boundaries: Reflect on how you prefer to spend your time, including your need for alone time versus social interaction.

Communicating Boundaries with Clarity and Respect

Once you've established your boundaries, the next step is communicating them. It's about finding that sweet spot where you're neither a pushover nor a fortress but a clear, assertive communicator.

Use "I" statements: Instead of saying, "You're always calling me late at night," try "I need quiet time in the evenings to unwind, so I'd prefer if we could talk earlier."

Be direct but gentle: Sugarcoating can muddy the waters, making your boundaries unclear. Be straightforward about your needs, but choose words that convey respect and understanding.

Practice ahead: If you're nervous about setting a boundary, rehearse what you want to say. It can help you convey your message more confidently.

Respecting and Responding to Others' Boundaries

Extending the same courtesy to others is crucial if you wish your boundaries to be respected. Recognizing and honoring someone else's boundaries shows that you value and respect them as individuals.

Listen actively: When someone is communicating their boundaries, give them your full attention. This demonstrates that you take their needs seriously.

Ask for clarification: If you're unsure about someone's boundaries, don't guess. Ask them to clarify, showing that you respect their limits.

Gracefully accept adjustments: People's boundaries can change, and they may need to set new ones with you. Approach these adjustments with understanding and flexibility.

Navigating the landscape of personal boundaries can sometimes feel like tiptoeing through a minefield, worried about every step. Yet, embracing the practice of setting, communicating, and respecting boundaries transforms that minefield into a garden. It becomes a place where relationships can flourish, rooted in mutual respect and understanding, where each individual feels valued and heard. This garden doesn't just bloom overnight. It requires patience, care, and the occasional pruning. Still, the result–a landscape of thriving, healthy relationships–is undeniably worth the effort.

6.4 Navigating Conflicts with Compassion and Patience

Have you ever tried skimming stones across the water? Each stone creates ripples that intersect with others, creating a beautifully complex pattern. Consider each stone a word, action, or misunderstanding in our relationships. Like those stones, they can stir up conflicts, sending ripples through our calm waters. With mindful wisdom, we can navigate these ripples without capsizing the boat.

Unearthing the Roots of Conflict

A simple truth lies at the heart of most clashes: they're often not about what's on the surface. Dig deeper and discover unmet needs, desires, or expectations. Misunderstandings act like fuel on the fire, transforming tiny sparks into blazing arguments. Recognizing these underlying causes isn't just about solving the immediate issue; it's about understanding each other deeper, ensuring smoother sailing ahead.

To do this, try to:

Keep an open mind, remembering there's always more to the story than what meets the eye.

Ask questions to uncover the real issues rather than making assumptions. Look beyond the immediate conflict to identify patterns indicating deeper issues.

Mindful-inspired Conflict Resolution

When smoothing over disputes, mindfulness offers a toolbox brimming with empathy, compassion, and mutual respect. These aren't just fluffy concepts but practical tools that transform a potential battleground into a meeting of minds.

Here's how you can apply them:

Approach the situation empathetically, striving to see things from the other person's perspective. This doesn't mean you have to agree, but understanding their viewpoint can pave the way for compromise.

Show compassion by acknowledging their feelings and offering support. Sometimes, just feeling heard can diffuse tension.

Maintain mutual respect, even in the heat of the moment. Remember, it's possible to disagree without diminishing the other person's dignity.

The Power of Patience in Resolving Disputes

If there's one thing more challenging than resolving conflicts, it's doing so with patience. In our fast-paced world, we want solutions yesterday, but proper resolution often requires giving things time to unfold naturally. Patience allows for reflection, a cooling-off period where the intensity of emotions can subside, making way for clearer thinking.
To cultivate patience:

Remind yourself that immediate solutions are only sometimes the best ones. Sometimes, sleeping on it can bring new insights.

Recognize and manage your impatience. If you're feeling antsy, take a few deep breaths or walk to clear your head.

Set realistic expectations about the resolution process. Understanding that some conflicts take time can help you maintain your composure.

Forgiveness and Reconciliation

The final puzzle piece is forgiveness, a concept that's easier said than done. Yet, it's a critical step in moving forward from conflict with a sense of peace and closure. Forgiveness isn't about condoning what happened or forgetting the hurt. It's about releasing past grievances' hold on you, freeing up space for healing and growth.

Engaging in forgiveness means:

Acknowledging the hurt and the part each person played in the conflict. This isn't about assigning blame but about owning your experiences. Deciding to let go of anger and resentment is a gift you give yourself that can lift a weight off your shoulders.

We are opening the door to reconciliation. While forgiveness is internal, reconciliation involves both parties coming together to rebuild trust and understanding.

Conflicts are inevitable in personal relationships, like ripples when stones skip across the water. But with compassion, patience, and generous forgiveness, we can navigate these challenges, ensuring that the ripples they create add to the beauty of our connections rather than disturbing the peace. It's about embracing the messiness, the imperfections, and the misunderstandings and seeing them as opportunities for growth, learning, and deeper bonds.

6.5 The Importance of Solo Time for Relationship Health

Carving out a slice of solitude is at odds with nurturing deep connections. Yet, in these quiet moments alone, the seeds of self-awareness and personal growth are sown, setting the stage for healthier, more vibrant relationships. Think of solo time as the soil from which a well-rounded, introspective self emerges, ready to engage more fully and meaningfully with others.

Embracing Solitude for Personal Growth

Solitude offers a unique lens through which we can view ourselves and our place in the world unclouded by the immediate demands or opinions of others. It's a state of being that invites introspection and self-discovery, allowing us to align our actions and choices with our deepest values and aspirations. This alignment enriches our sense of self and enhances how we show up in our relationships, grounded in a strong sense of identity and purpose.

Engage in journaling to explore your thoughts and feelings, tracing patterns illuminating your underlying motivations and desires.

Meditation or mindful breathing can deepen one's connection to the present moment, fostering a sense of inner peace that one brings back to one's interactions with others.

Balancing Solo Time and Togetherness

Finding equilibrium between solitude and social interaction is akin to mixing the perfect cocktail–too much of one ingredient can throw off the entire experience. The key is to listen to your needs and communicate them clearly, ensuring that time spent alone and with loved ones contributes to the richness of your life.
Schedule regular "me time" just as you would a date night or family outing, making it a non-negotiable part of your routine.
Stay attuned to the ebb and flow of your need for solitude, recognizing when it's time to recharge alone and when it's time to seek the company of others.

Activities for Productive Solo Time

The quality of your alone time matters. It's not just about being by yourself but about engaging in activities that replenish your spirit, spark your creativity, and broaden your horizons.

Pursue a hobby that brings you joy, whether painting, gardening, or playing an instrument. These activities offer a sense of accomplishment and pleasure that enhances your well-being.

Exploring nature through a leisurely walk in the park or a challenging hike can ground you at the moment and provide a fresh perspective on life's challenges.

Communicating the Need for Solo Time

Openly discussing your need for solitude can be tricky, especially if loved ones fear being pushed away. Yet, honest communication about why solo time is essential to your well-being strengthens understanding and respect within your relationships.

Frame the conversation around the benefits, explaining how solitude enriches your life and, by extension, your relationships.

Reassure loved ones that your desire for alone time is not a reflection of your feelings for them but a way to be your best self when you're together.

Propose specific plans for reconnecting afterward, demonstrating that your relationship remains a priority.

In weaving the threads of solitude into the fabric of our lives, we cultivate a deeper relationship with ourselves and lay the groundwork for more authentic, fulfilling connections with others. Solo time, far from being a sign of withdrawal, is a proactive step toward personal and relational health, a testament to the understanding that to love others well, we must first love and know ourselves.

So remember: the dance between solitude and togetherness is ongoing, a rhythm that shapes the melody of our lives. We find harmony in embracing the quiet moments alone and the shared experiences with loved ones. This balance enriches every note of our existence. With this foundation of self-awareness and intentional solitude, we're poised to explore the further intricacies of personal growth and how it radiates outwards, touching every aspect of our lives.

CHAPTER 7

WATCHING THE CLOCK

"All we have to decide is what to do with the time that is given us."

J. R. R. Tolkien

Have you ever caught yourself muttering, "I wish I had more hours in the day"? You're trying to rest, but your mind races with unchecked to-do lists, or you're staring at your coffee, wondering if it has the magic to stretch time.

I remember a busy Monday in a stressful job. I reached the end of the day and looked at everything I had checked off my to-do list. I was overjoyed; I had crushed the day and felt elated. I should have shut down my computer and gone home, but I didn't. I refreshed my email and watched an avalanche of new messages pile into my inbox, each with a new task. Within two minutes, my to-do list was full again, and I was frustrated. I wanted another five hours in the day. I didn't understand that the work never stops, and I was on my way to burnout.

7.1 Reframing Time

The clock ticks the same for everyone, from the CEO to the barista at your favorite coffee shop. Yet, how we perceive those ticks can differ wildly. I used to view times as a relentless taskmaster; it's one of the factors that led me to burnout. I'm now viewing time as a stream. Sometimes, I swim with the current, and other times, I swim against it, but often, I float, letting the water take me. My day's best moments are those floating moments, finding peace in the flow. It's not about adding more to your day but enriching it. Here are some mindfulness moments you can include in your day.

Morning ritual: While your coffee brews, stand by the window and watch the world wake up for two minutes. Simply be still and focus on the moment.

The commute: Stuck in traffic or waiting for a train? That's not wasted time; it's an opportunity. Turn off the radio. Focus on your breathing. Look at what's around you; take in the sights, sounds, and smells.

While doing chores: Washing dishes? Feel the water's temperature and the texture of the bubbles. You're not just cleaning dishes; you're practicing mindfulness.

Mindful To-do

Putting mindfulness on your to-do list might seem counterintuitive, like trying to schedule spontaneity. Yet, it's about giving mindfulness the same importance as your other non-negotiables. The joy of these practices lies in their simplicity and scalability. You don't need an hour; a minute can suffice. These micro-practices are like secret weapons, tucked away in your day, ready to deploy when stress levels rise.

Micro-practices for Busy Schedules

Set reminders: A sticky note on your bathroom mirror with "Breathe" can be a simple prompt.

Allocating time: Dedicate the first five minutes of your lunch break to simply sitting and breathing. No scrolling, no chatting. Just you and your breath.

One-minute breathing: Before you jump into your next task, take a minute. Breathe deeply, in through the nose, out through the mouth. Feel the air, the expansion of your lungs. One minute, and you're reset. Gratitude list: Waiting for a file to download? Jot down three things you're grateful for today. Gratitude is a cornerstone of mindfulness, a quick pathway back to the present.

Sensory check-in: This can be done anywhere, anytime.

Pause: Notice five things you can see, four you can touch, three you can hear, two you can smell, and one you can taste. It's a fast track to mindfulness, grounding you in the now.

Incorporating mindfulness into your life isn't about carving out chunks of your day; it's about stitching moments into the fabric of your daily routine. It's recognizing that while you might not be able to control the chaos around you, you can control your response. You're navigating your day more calmly and transforming your relationship by reframing your perception of time, integrating mindfulness into everyday tasks, prioritizing these practices, and embracing micro-practices. It's about making peace with the clock, one moment at a time.

7.2 "This Won't Solve My Problems": Understanding the Role of Mindfulness

First, being mindful isn't a magic wand. It won't make your challenges vanish into thin air. But let's be honest: Your other techniques have yet to work, and you're staring at burnout.

Developing mindfulness is akin to cleaning your glasses; you suddenly see your problems with a missing clarity. It's about adjusting the lenses through which you view your life, transforming obstacles into manageable tasks. This perspective shift doesn't diminish the problems but empowers you to handle them with a calm, steady hand.

Life's hurdles remain, but you're no longer dodging bullets in a blind panic. You're making strategic moves, conserving energy, and finding more imaginative, serene ways to tackle them head-on.

Addressing Skepticism with Science

For the skeptics among us, let's talk science. Research in neuroscience and psychology backs up the benefits of mindfulness and meditation. Studies have shown that these practices can rewire the brain, strengthening areas responsible for attention, emotional regulation, and stress management. MRI scans of regular meditators reveal enhanced connectivity in brain regions linked to self-awareness and empathy, alongside a reduction in areas associated with anxiety and stress.

One study found that just eight weeks of mindfulness practice was enough to bring about significant changes in the brain, correlating with reduced stress levels and improved emotional well-being. This isn't just feel-good folklore; it's hard science showing how mindful practices can be a game-changer in your problem-solving repertoire.

In navigating the waters of life, I'm not promising a storm-free voyage. But mindfulness offers the skill to sail through storms without losing your cool, find your balance amidst turbulence, and see the sun peeking through the clouds, even in the heart of the storm. It's about recognizing that while you may not control the wind, you can constantly adjust your sails, turning challenges into opportunities for growth, learning, and perhaps peace.

7.3 "I've Tried Before and Failed": Overcoming Past Setbacks

So, you tried mindfulness, and it felt like trying to juggle with your feet–a bit of a flop. Maybe you figured meditation would instantly quiet your mind, but you found yourself planning dinner instead. Or perhaps those attempts at mindfulness left you more aware of your boredom than a newfound inner peace. Let's get one thing straight: hitting a snag isn't a sign to throw in the towel. It's simply part of the journey.

Understanding the Nature of Practice

Think of these habits as learning to ride a bike. Those first few tries? You're bound to wobble, maybe even take a spill. But with each attempt, you're getting a feel for the balance, the motion, and how to steer. It's not about reaching a flawless state; it's about getting better at finding your balance, even if you occasionally tip over. So, when a mindful practice doesn't stick the first time or the tenth, it's not failure. It's you figuring out how to ride this bike uniquely.

Personalizing the Practice

The beauty of these practices is their flexibility. They're like water – meant to flow into the crevices of your life, filling up spaces you didn't know needed attention.

For the early riser: If dawn is your time, incorporate a few minutes of silence each morning. Let the first light be your meditation.

Night owls, unite: Use those quiet evening hours for a reflective journaling session. Let the stillness of the night guide your thoughts.

On-the-go: Always running from one thing to the next? Pause between tasks for three deep breaths. That's your mindfulness moment.
Celebrating Small Victories

In the grand tapestry of life, the small threads – the tiny, seemingly insignificant moments – create the rich, vibrant picture. Each time you catch yourself automatically taking a deep breath to release tension, that's a win. When you find yourself fully absorbed in a mundane task, noticing its rhythm and texture, that's mindfulness weaving its way into your life.

Acknowledge the effort: Simply taking time for mindfulness practices, no matter the outcome, is a step worth celebrating.

Notice the shifts: You may be more patient in the morning traffic or find bits of joy in unexpected places. These are the subtle signs of your mindfulness practice taking root.

Share your journey: Sometimes, articulating your progress to someone else can make it more real. It's a way of acknowledging your path, with all its twists and turns.

This isn't about adding more items to your to-do list; it's about embracing each moment as another chance to practice, learn, and grow. So, dust off from those setbacks, adjust your grip on the handlebars, and pedal forward. Remember, every ride gets a bit smoother, and soon, you'll find your flow, cruising down the path with the wind in your hair, a smile on your face, and a heart full of joy.

7.4 "Mindfulness Is Not for Someone Like Me": Breaking Down Stereotypes

Flip through any magazine or scroll through your social feeds, and you might think mindfulness is the exclusive domain of the ultra-flexible or those with an abundance of spare time to sit cross-legged atop mountains at sunrise. But honestly, mindfulness doesn't care about your flexibility, schedule, or whether you can tell a chakra from a chimichanga. It's far more democratic than that. So, let's toss out those old stereotypes and look at who can benefit from mindfulness.

Challenging Stereotypes

The stereotype that you must fit a specific mold to practice mindfulness is as outdated as flip phones. Here are some of the most common myths:

Myth: Mindfulness is only for those who are spiritually inclined.

Reality: Mindfulness is about finding calm and clarity, whether you're spiritual or as secular as they come.

Myth: You need tons of free time to dedicate to mindfulness practices.

Reality: Snatching moments for mindfulness can be as simple as taking a few deep breaths during your coffee break.

Myth: Mindfulness practices require silence and solitude
.

Reality: You can practice mindfulness anywhere – in the middle of a hectic day or while doing laundry.

Customizing Mindfulness to Fit Your Life

The exciting part is molding mindfulness practices to fit into your unique life's contours. It's about making mindfulness your own, not shoehorning your life into a preconceived notion of what it 'should' be. Start where you are: If sitting silently isn't your thing, try a walking meditation or mindful cooking.

Use what you've got: No need for Himalayan singing bowls; the hum of city traffic or the rhythm of your breath can serve as focal points for mindfulness.

Align with your interests: Do you love music? Try focusing entirely on a song, immersing yourself in each note and lyric as a form of meditation. Mindfulness is not a one-size-fits-all t-shirt but a tailor-made suit that fits the unique shape of your life and experiences. It's about finding your version of peace and mindfulness, whether in the quiet of dawn or the chaos of a city street. So, if you've ever thought, "Mindfulness isn't for someone like me," it might be time to reconsider. Because in its most pure form, it is about embracing life with awareness, acceptance, and a sense of calm – and that's a fit for anyone.

7.5 "I Can't Sit Still": Mindfulness for the Restless Mind and Body

So, you're the type whose legs start bouncing the moment you sit down or whose mind races faster than a high-speed train the second you try to "relax." Sitting through a meditation session is as appealing as watching paint dry. But hold up–this doesn't mean mindfulness is out of your league. It's all about finding the right fit that matches your vibe while still nudging you into a state of calm and mindfulness. Here's how to weave mindfulness into the fabric of your kinetic life without feeling like you've been strapped to a chair.

Movement-based practices

Who said mindfulness has to be a static affair? The world's your playground, and there are myriad ways to engage in mindfulness while keeping your body in motion.

Walking meditation is for those who prefer motion. Next time you're walking, anywhere really, pay attention to each step, the feel of the ground under your feet, and the rhythm of your strides. It's a valid and valuable form of meditation.

Yoga for every mood: Sure, yoga's known for its calming effects, but there are dynamic forms, too. Have you ever tried power yoga? It's got all the mindfulness you'd want but with a tempo that keeps up with your energy.

Short-duration practices

Starting small doesn't just apply to portions at dinner. With mindfulness, especially for the fidgeters among us, short bursts of practice can be the way to go.

Just a minute: Focusing on your breath for just 60 seconds can do wonders. Do it while waiting for your computer to boot or the kettle to boil. It's about quality, not quantity.

The five-breath escape: Feel that restlessness kicking in? Pause and take five deep breaths. Focus on the in and out. You've just practiced mindfulness without having to clear your schedule.

Engaging the senses

Sometimes, the best way to quiet the mind is to give it something else to focus on, something tangible. This is where your senses come in.

Mindful eating: Turn your next snack into a mindfulness session. Notice the texture, the taste, and the aroma. Eating slowly and savoring each bite can be a form of meditation that doesn't feel like one.
Nature observation: Next time you're outside, really look around. Notice the colors of the leaves, the patterns of the clouds, and the way

the light plays on surfaces. It's mindfulness in disguise, perfect for those who find stillness challenging.

Understanding the value of discomfort

Here's an idea I used to hate: Discomfort isn't your enemy; it's packed with potential. That's not a failure when you fidget during a short meditation or feel antsy during a slow yoga flow. That's an opportunity knocking.

Lean into it: Instead of immediately shifting to find comfort, stay with the discomfort for a moment longer each time. In these moments, you learn about yourself, your limits, and how you might gently expand them.

Reflect on the experience: After sitting with discomfort, take a moment to think about it. What was it like? Did it change over time? Often, you'll find the pain lessens, teaching you about impermanence and resilience. As we wrap up, remember that mindfulness doesn't demand a complete lifestyle overhaul. It's about sprinkling it and calm into your day, whether you're on the move or taking a moment to breathe. It's about making peace with the present, one step, one breath, one bite at a time. And all of these little steps help us stop burnout.

CHAPTER 8

WHOLE LIFE MINDFULNESS

"Training your mind to be the present moment is the number one key to making healthier choices."

– Susan Albers.

As we discussed in this book, mindfulness is critical in the journey to stop burnout. The paths to mindfulness vary as much as the people who walk them. Some stumbled upon it while seeking relief from the unbearable weight of stress and anxiety. Others were drawn to it out of curiosity, a desire for deeper self-understanding, or the need to find balance in their fast-paced lives. Each story is a testament to the power of mindfulness practices to catalyze profound personal transformations.

8.1 The Ripple Effect: How Your Peace Influences Others

When you incorporate mindfulness into your daily life, it's like tossing a pebble into a pond. The ripples extend far beyond the initial splash, touching shores you might not even see. You become a walking, talking demonstration of mindfulness power, which can spark curiosity in those around you and nudge them toward exploring mindfulness and stress management techniques.

Imagine you're the calm in the eye of the storm at work, navigating deadlines and demands with a cool head while others are concerned. People notice. They see you taking those five-minute meditation breaks or handling conflict with a level of patience that's borderline superhero. And they start asking questions, wondering what your secret is. This is your cue to share, not preach, how mindfulness practices help you stay anchored. It's about showing, not telling. Your lived experience serves as a powerful, silent invitation for others.

Improving Relationships Through Mindfulness

Think about the last time you disagreed with someone close to you. The kind where emotions run high, and everything feels a bit too intense. Integrating mindfulness into your life can transform these moments. Suddenly, you find yourself listening more and reacting less. You're empathizing and truly understanding where the other person is coming from, and this shifts the entire dynamic. Conversations flow, you find common ground faster, and the bond deepens. It's like mindfulness gives you a new set of tools for your relationship toolbox, which is all about building bridges rather than walls.

Creating a Mindfulness Environment

Here's a fun experiment: create a mindfulness corner in your home or workspace. It doesn't have to be elaborate–a plant, a comfortable chair, and maybe a tiny collection of calming images or objects. This little oasis becomes a visual cue to breathe and center yourself. But its effects can ripple out, influencing the whole space. Others might be drawn to it, asking questions or creating mindfulness nooks. Before you know it, you've started a trend, turning your home or office into a network of mini-sanctuaries. It's about crafting spaces that breathe peace, inviting everyone to pause and find a moment of calm.

Encouraging Collective Mindfulness Practices

Something is compelling about shared mindfulness practices. They can turn a group of individuals into a connected, cohesive unit, all moving together toward greater mindfulness and stress reduction. Here are a few ways to weave collective mindfulness practices into your life:

Family Mindfulness Time: Dedicate a few minutes each evening for family meditation or mindful breathing. It can be a serene bookend to the day, a chance for everyone to gather and release the day's stresses together.

Mindful Meetings: You could start meetings at work with a minute of silent reflection. This would center the group, clear the mental clutter, and set a focused tone for the discussion.

Community Mindfulness Events: Organize a weekly meditation meet-up in your local park or community center. It's a great way to build connections, share practices, and create a communal sense of peace and well-being.

Incorporating mindfulness into your life isn't just about personal transformation. It's about setting off a chain reaction, a series of ripples that extend outward, touching the lives of those around you profoundly. It's about becoming a beacon of calm, inspiration and a catalyst for collective well-being. Through simple acts and shared practices, you can help foster environments where peace and mindfulness aren't just individual pursuits but a shared journey, enriching your life and the lives of everyone around you.

8.2 Mindfulness as a Philosophy for Life, Not Just Stress Management

Diving into mindfulness is like discovering a new color you never knew existed. Suddenly, you see it everywhere, changing how you look at the world. It's not just a stress buster; it's a lens that brings life into sharper focus, coloring your decisions, actions, and sense of purpose with more prosperous, vibrant hues. Let's peel back the layers and see how mindfulness can infuse every aspect of your life with clarity, compassion, and intention.

Broadening the Definition of Mindfulness

At its core, mindfulness is about more than just chilling out. It's a way of being, thinking, and acting that can touch every corner of your life. From how you sip your morning coffee to navigating complex challenges at work, mindfulness principles offer a guiding light. It's about presence, acceptance, and gracefully moving through the world. This isn't about detaching from life's ups and downs but engaging with them more fully, with a heart and mind open to whatever comes your way.

Integrating Mindfulness into Decision-Making

Imagine you're at a crossroads, each path leading to wildly different horizons. How do you choose? Here's where mindfulness shines. It encourages you to pause, breathe, and connect with a more profound sense of intuition and wisdom. Decisions become less about what's expected or feared and more about what aligns with your most authentic self. Whether deciding on a career move, a relationship, or a personal goal, mindfulness principles can help you weigh your options with a balanced mind and a compassionate heart.

Mindful weighing of options: Before jumping to conclusions, consider each choice, reflecting on how it aligns with your core values and long-term vision.

Embracing uncertainty: Sometimes, the fear of making the wrong choice can paralyze you. Mindfulness teaches you to embrace the unknown, making peace with the fact that there's beauty and growth to be found in uncertainty.

Compassionate considerations: When your decisions impact others, mindfulness prompts you to consider their well-being alongside your own, fostering kind and fair decisions.

Mindfulness and the Pursuit of Purpose

Finding your purpose is like tuning an instrument. Everything resonates when it's in tune, creating a harmony between what you do and who you are. Mindfulness practices help you tune into your life's purpose by quieting the external noise, allowing you to listen more deeply to your inner voice. This isn't about grandiose achievements or societal benchmarks of success but finding meaning and satisfaction in the every day, in ways big and small.

Reflection and meditation: These practices can be your compass, helping you navigate toward activities and goals that light you up from the inside.

Serving others: Mindfulness emphasizes the interconnection of all things, guiding you towards purposes that serve your fulfillment and the well-being of others and the world.

Sustaining a Lifelong Mindfulness Practice

Like any meaningful relationship, your connection with mindfulness will evolve. What starts as a simple stress management tool can blossom into a lifelong journey of discovery, growth, and fulfillment. Keeping your mindfulness practice vibrant and relevant over the years requires attention, intention, and a willingness to adapt.

Regular check-ins: Periodically take stock of your practice. What's working? What feels stale? This isn't about rigid adherence to a routine but staying true to mindfulness's ideas of flow and flexibility.

Introduce new elements: Just as you'd spice up your cooking with new flavors, don't be afraid to mix new practices into your mindfulness routine. Exploring meditation techniques and mindfulness exercises or attending retreats can keep your practice fresh and engaging.

Embrace life's changes: As you grow and change, so will your needs and challenges. What served you well in one season of life might not fit in another. Adjusting your practice to meet your evolving needs keeps it relevant and personal.

Immersing yourself in mindfulness as a philosophy for life offers a more prosperous, more nuanced way to navigate the world. It's about finding depth in simplicity, strength in vulnerability, and profound peace amid life's inevitable storms. Mindfulness invites you to slow down, breathe deeply, and open your eyes to the wonder and beauty around you daily. It's a journey that promises no final destination, only an ever-deepening appreciation for the art of living well.

8.3 Maintaining Your Mindfulness Practice in Times of Change

Life's like surfing. Some days, you're crushing it, nailing tricks like a pro. Other days? You're collapsing on the beach, coughing up salt water. But here's the thing: it's all part of the ride, especially when life decides to shake things up–job shifts, moving cities, or even just the world choosing to throw a curveball our way. Here's how you keep your mindfulness vibe strong, no matter what kind of grind you face.

Mindfulness in the Face of Adversity

When the going gets tough, the tough get going, right? But sometimes, just plowing through isn't enough. Mindfulness offers a steadier, more balanced way to handle life's upheavals.

Find your anchor: When everything feels spinning, find one practice that keeps you grounded. It could be a five-minute meditation each morning or a nightly gratitude list. Could you keep it simple and make it stick?

Ride the wave: Think of challenges like waves. You can fight them, sure, but often, it's about finding the rhythm, riding them out. Use your mindfulness practice to stay flexible and flow with what life tosses your way rather than getting knocked down.

Turn to the page: Journaling isn't just for poets. It's a powerful tool for processing feelings, especially during tough times. Scribble, doodle, vent–getting it down on paper can help make sense of the chaos.

Adapting Practices for Life Stages

Just like your taste in music evolves (admit it, your playlist isn't what it was five years ago), your mindfulness practice must also flow with the changes. Each stage of life sings a different tune, and your mindfulness practice should harmonize with that.

Young adulthood: This stage is about discovery and is often with change. Short, mobile meditation apps can fit well here, offering a quick mindfulness fix on the move.

Mid-life: Responsibilities often peak here, with career and family in the mix. Mindful moments of solitude, like early morning or late at night, can offer the calm you need.

Later years: This time might bring more free hours. It's perfect for diving deeper, joining a meditation group, or exploring longer, more reflective practices.

The Role of Community in Sustaining Practice

Ever notice how laughs are louder in a group? Mindfulness is like that. It sticks better with people who get it and ride the same wave. Finding or building a community keeps the motivation and makes the practice richer.

Virtual tribes: Thanks to the digital age, you're never solo. Online meditation groups, forums, or social media can link you with fellow mindfulness seekers.

Local gatherings: Nothing beats the in-person vibe. Check out local yoga studios, meditation centers, or even community boards for groups or events.

Create your circle: Need help finding what you need? Start your group. Invite friends for a weekly meditation meet-up in the park or start a mindfulness book club. Sometimes, the best communities are the ones we build ourselves.

Here's a secret: change isn't just something to get through; it's ripe with possibilities. The universe says, "Hey, time to shake things up." Mindfulness is not about resisting change; it's about diving in, finding the silver lining, the growth waiting on the other side.

Shift your lens: Instead of seeing change as a threat, try viewing it as a chance to evolve. Ask yourself, "What can I learn here? How can I grow?"

Stay open: Mindfulness teaches us to approach life with openness and curiosity. Apply that to change. Be curious about where this new path might lead and what new doors might open.

Lean into the discomfort: Change can be uncomfortable and even scary. But remember, growth often happens outside our comfort zones. Use your mindfulness practice to stay present in the discomfort and explore it rather than run from it.

Navigating life's changes with mindfulness doesn't mean you won't face challenges or have moments of doubt. What it does mean is that you've got a set of tools to help you deal with those challenges more effectively. It's about staying grounded when the world's shifting, finding peace amid upheaval, and seeing change not as an end but as a beginning. It's about riding that skateboard through life, knowing that you might fall, but you've also got what it takes to get back up, adjust your stance, and keep cruising.

8.4 The Journey Continues: Evolving Your Mindful Practice

The path of mindfulness isn't a straight line; it's more like a meandering river, ever-changing as it flows through the landscape of your life. Recognizing that your mindfulness practice will morph, grow, and shift alongside you is crucial. It's not about sticking rigidly to one practice but allowing your engagement with mindfulness to be as dynamic and multifaceted as you are.

The Evolving Nature of Mindfulness

Your relationship with mindfulness will twist and turn, ebb and flow. Initially, it might have been a life raft in stormy seas, a way to find calm amidst chaos. As the skies clear and you navigate smoother waters, mindfulness becomes a tool for exploration, a way to dive deeper into the waters of self-discovery and personal growth. It's all part of adapting your practice as your needs, interests, and circumstances evolve.

Learning from Setbacks

Hitting a rough patch in your mindfulness practice isn't a sign of failure; it's an opportunity for growth. Maybe you've found your interest waning, or life's busyness has edged out your dedicated mindfulness time. Instead of beating yourself up, approach these moments with curiosity and compassion. What's at the root of this shift? Is it a signal that your practice needs to evolve or a reminder to recommit to the fundamentals? Each setback is a chance to learn more about yourself and to refine and adjust your practice in ways that align with your current path.

Setting Intentions for Continued Growth

Looking forward is vital to keeping your mindfulness practice alive and vibrant. Setting intentions isn't about creating rigid goals but rather establishing a direction, an area of focus that can guide your exploration and growth. You should deepen your understanding of mindfulness science or aim to integrate mindfulness more fully into your daily interactions. By setting these intentions, you create a framework for your practice. This scaffold supports your journey while allowing the flexibility for unexpected discoveries and detours.

As you continue to weave mindfulness into the fabric of your existence, remember that the journey itself is what matters. It's a path of discovery, challenges, and growth, a way of living that brings depth, clarity, and peace to every moment. Your practice will change because you are changing, and that's exactly as it should be. Let your mindfulness journey reflect who you are and who you're becoming, a dynamic dance with life that brings you ever closer to your most authentic self.

CONCLUSION

"If we start being honest about our pain, our anger, and our shortcomings instead of pretending they don't exist, then maybe we'll leave the world a better place than we found it."

– Russell Wilson

Well, my friend, we've been on quite the adventure together, haven't we? From the initial realization that stress is pulling the strings on our well-being and joy to the intricate journey of weaving mindfulness into the fabric of our everyday routines, we have been painting the bigger picture of a life transformed by mindfulness. It's been confirmed, and I hope you've had as many "aha!" moments as I did when I first stumbled down this rabbit hole.

Let's not forget the juicy bits we've picked up along the way - the understanding that stress isn't just an annoying buzz in our ears but a call to action; the revelation that mindfulness practices aren't just for the enlightened few living atop a mountain but are as accessible as your next breath; and the realization that setting boundaries, saying "no," and prioritizing self-care aren't selfish acts, but radical acts of self-love. What are the long-term benefits? Oh, they're the real deal. Imagine navigating life's ups and downs with grace, your mental and emotional health as sturdy as a centuries-old oak, your relationships deepening, and your professional life flourishing because you're present and focused. It's not a pipe dream; it's the destination of our journey.

Don't let the fear of not "doing it right" hold you back. Start small. Pick one or two practices that resonated with you and weave them into the fabric of your day. Remember, the path to stopping burnout is as unique as you are, evolving and adapting as you do.

This isn't an exclusive club. Whether you're a stressed-out CEO, a busy parent, or a student juggling a thousand things - these practices are your ticket to a more balanced, peaceful existence. And why go alone when you can join or create a mindfulness community? Sharing the journey makes the load lighter and the laughs louder.

Patience and persistence, my friend. If you hit a bump or take a detour, welcome it. It's all part of the glorious, messy process of growth. The version of you that emerges will be all the richer for it.

As we wrap up this wild ride, I want to leave you with a vision - a life where stress doesn't call the shots, where each moment is lived fully, and where peace and fulfillment aren't just words in a self-help book but your lived reality. It's within reach. All it takes is that first step to say, "Yes, I'm doing this."

From the bottom of my heart, this book has lit a spark in you, offering tools and practices, hope, and a sense of connection. My journey with mindfulness has been transformative in ways I could never have imagined, and I'm so excited for you to experience your transformation. Here's to beating stress and stopping burnout. You've got this
.

With love,

Patrick

P.S. Keep reading for 50 mindful affirmations to get you started.

Affirmations

This will be a mindful and at peace year. It will be a year of strength, power, health and happiness. At the end of the year I will be wealthier and more content. My relationship with my family and friends will be filled with mindfulness and peace.

At the start of the year, I am making a conscious decision to let go of last year and focus on the year ahead. Each day, I will commit to my goals, focus my energy and crush my barriers. Let the year ahead understand that I am mindful and at peace.

This year, I will ensure my mind is fighting fit and powerful. I will focus my mind on what truly matters to me and let the bullshit drop away. I will give my mind what it needs to be strong and not think about any garbage. My mind understands that I am mindful and at peace.

This year, I acknowledge that I am worthy of love, I am worthy of happiness, and I am worthy of peace. I will continue on my journey to these things and will accept nothing less than that in my life because I am mindful and at peace.

This year, I will clearly mark out my goals. I will visualise them, declare them and give my all to achieve them. I will not create excuses; I will not be lame. I will accept the responsibility I have for achieving my goals because I am mindful and at peace.

As I kick off this new year with my family, I'm locking in on fortifying our connections, injecting positive vibes into our shared adventures, and smashing through any obstacles that dare cross our path. Let the world take notice that we're an unstoppable force, bound together by strength, love, and unyielding resolve. Together, we are mindful and at peace.

This year, I am a steadfast and loyal friend, committed to strengthening the bonds of brotherhood. My actions reflect genuine care and support, creating a foundation of trust that withstands the tests of time. I embrace the growth of our friendship, fostering an environment where we can thrive together sharing laughter, challenges, and triumphs. I am a mindful and at peace friend.

This year, I am a person of character. I am dedicated to maintaining my integrity. I will be a person of my word in a world that wants me to lie and cheat. I will not take the easy path but the one that most reflects who I am because I am mindful and at peace.

This year, I am a man of unwavering inner strength. In the face of challenges, I stand tall, drawing power from the resilience within me. My spirit is unbreakable, my resolve unshakeable. I confront adversity with courage, transforming obstacles into stepping stones on my journey because I am mindful and at peace.

This year I will see every trial as an opportunity to tap into the well of strength that resides deep within. I trust in my capabilities, knowing that I possess the fortitude to overcome any obstacle. My inner strength will lead me through life's storms. It is a force that propels me toward success and fulfilment because I am mindful and at peace.

This year will be a testament to the power that lies within me. With each trial, I emerge stronger, more resilient, and more deeply connected to the unyielding core of my being because I am mindful and at peace.

This year I will cultivate a sanctuary of inner peace within myself, a tranquil haven that remains unshaken by the chaos of the world. In the midst of life's turbulence, I find solace in the depths of my being, where serenity resides. And it will be mindful and at peace.

Through mindfulness and self-awareness, I embrace the present moment this year. I do it with acceptance and gratitude, releasing the burdens of the past and the anxieties of the future. My inner peace is a flashlight, illuminating the path to harmony and balance in all aspects of my life and it is mindful and at peace.

I nurture compassion and forgiveness toward myself and others, this year. I foster a sense of interconnectedness with people today that transcends conflict and division. With each breath, I draw in peace, allowing it to permeate every fiber of my being, and with each exhale, I release tension and negativity because I am mindful and at peace.

This year, I am the embodiment of tranquillity, radiating calmness and serenity to the world around me, inspiring others to find their own inner peace amidst the tumult of life and together we will be mindful and at peace.

This year, I embody a healthy mindset, cultivating thoughts that empower and inspire. I choose optimism over doubt, resilience over despair, and growth over stagnation. My mind is a fertile ground for positivity and possibility, where challenges are viewed as opportunities for learning and self-discovery because I am mindful and at peace.

This year, I embrace a mindset of abundance, recognizing the limitless potential within myself and the world. I prioritize self-care, nurturing my mental and emotional well-being with mindfulness and compassion. I release negativity and cultivate gratitude, acknowledging the abundance in my life. In the face of setbacks, I see them as temporary detours rather than insurmountable obstacles because I am mindful and at peace.

My healthy mindset fuels my actions, guiding me toward choices that promote physical, mental, and emotional well-being. I am the architect of my thoughts, creating a foundation for a fulfilling and purpose-driven life. Each day, I reaffirm my commitment to a healthy mindset, knowing that it is the key to unlocking my fullest potential and embracing a life of joy and fulfillment. I am mindful and at peace.

I am a bonfire of optimism, radiating positivity in every aspect of my life. I choose to see the bright side of every situation, understanding that challenges are opportunities in disguise and they are mindful and at peace.

My optimism is a powerful force that propels me forward, infusing my actions with hope and resilience. In the face of adversity, I maintain a positive outlook, confident that I can overcome any obstacle. I attract positivity into my life by focusing on solutions rather than problems, and by surrounding myself with uplifting energy. I am mindful and at peace.

Optimism is my default mindset, shaping my thoughts and actions to align with a future filled with possibilities. I believe in the inherent goodness of people and the potential for positive change. People are mindful and at peace.

Each day is a new canvas, and I paint it with the vibrant hues of optimism, creating a life rich in joy, gratitude, and boundless opportunities. My optimistic mindset is a magnetic force that attracts success, fulfillment, and a life filled with limitless potential. I am mindful and at peace.

I am a resilient force, capable of overcoming any obstacle that stands in my way. Challenges are not roadblocks but opportunities for growth and transformation. With unwavering determination, I face adversity head-on, turning setbacks into stepping stones toward success. I am mindful and at peace.

Each obstacle is a test of my strength, and I meet these tests with courage and perseverance. I embrace the lessons within challenges, extracting wisdom that propels me forward on my journey. No obstacle is insurmountable; I possess the tenacity to find creative solutions and the resilience to endure the journey. I am mindful and at peace.

I channel the power of perseverance, knowing that setbacks are temporary and do not define my ultimate path. Through focus, adaptability, and a positive mindset, I navigate the twists and turns of life with grace. I am not defined by the challenges I encounter; instead, I am shaped by my ability to overcome them. I am mindful and at peace.

Every obstacle becomes a stepping stone to a higher level of achievement, and with each triumph, I emerge stronger, wiser, and more equipped to conquer the next challenge on my journey for I am mindful and at peace.

I am a boundless wellspring of creativity, channeling innovative ideas and originality in every endeavor. My mind is a canvas, and I paint upon it with the vibrant strokes of imagination. I embrace the joy of exploration, welcoming the uncharted territories of inspiration. I am mindful and at peace.

Creativity flows through me effortlessly, sparking inventive solutions and novel perspectives. I see challenges as opportunities to express my creative genius, turning obstacles into gateways of innovation. In every project, I infuse a touch of uniqueness, leaving my mark as a creator because I am mindful and at peace.

I trust in the infinite possibilities of my imagination, allowing ideas to flow freely and manifest into reality. I cultivate a creative mindset, nourishing my creativity through curiosity, play, and an openness to the beauty of the unexpected, for I am mindful and at peace.

With each creative endeavor, I tap into the vast reservoir of my imagination, unlocking new dimensions of self-expression and ingenuity. I am a creator, and my creativity knows no bounds, shaping a world rich in originality, beauty, and endless possibilities. I am mindful and at peace.

I am a powerhouse of physical strength, a living testament to the potential of my body's capabilities. Through dedication and discipline, I sculpt and strengthen my physique, forging a temple of resilience and endurance. I am mindful and at peace.

I will exercise today. I push my limits, embracing the discomfort as a pathway to growth. My body is a reflection of the hard work and commitment I invest in my well-being. I fuel myself with nutritious choices, providing the energy needed to conquer challenges and exceed expectations. I am mindful and at peace.

Today, I understand that physical strength is not just a goal but a way of life for me. I revel in the vitality that surges through my muscles, fostering a sense of confidence and empowerment. I am in tune with my body, listening to its cues and nurturing it with rest and recovery. In moments of physical exertion, I discover the depths of my capabilities, pushing beyond boundaries and reaching new heights because I am mindful and at peace.

Today, I stand tall in my physical strength, embodying the harmony between my mind and body. With each stride, lift, and push, I celebrate the resilience and power that reside within me. I am mindful and at peace.

I am the steward of my physical health, nurturing my body with care and respect. I recognize that my well-being is a precious gift, and I honor it by making mindful choices that promote vitality and longevity because I am mindful and at peace.

Today, I nourish myself with wholesome foods, fueling my body with the nutrients it craves to thrive. Physical activity is not just a routine but a celebration of movement and strength. I embrace exercise as a cornerstone of my lifestyle, engaging in activities that invigorate my body and soul. I am mindful and at peace.

Today, I prioritize rest and recovery, honoring the rhythms of restorative sleep that rejuvenate my mind and body. I listen to my body's cues, acknowledging its need for balance and harmony. I approach health challenges with resilience and determination, seeking support and guidance when needed. I am mindful and at peace.

Each day is an opportunity to cultivate a healthier version of myself, one mindful choice at a time. I am the architect of my physical health, sculpting a life of vitality, resilience, and boundless energy. With each breath, I reaffirm my commitment to nurturing my body and honoring the temple that houses my spirit. I am mindful and at peace.

I am a magnet for wealth and abundance, and I create prosperity with purpose and intention. I recognize that wealth extends beyond mere financial gain; it encompasses a holistic abundance that enhances every aspect of my life, and it is mindful and at peace.

Today, I attract opportunities for financial growth and success through strategic planning, diligent effort, and a mindset of abundance. Challenges are stepping stones to wealth creation, learning valuable lessons that propel me forward. I am mindful and at peace.

I am resourceful and open-minded, exploring diverse income generation and investment avenues. My financial goals are clear, and I take consistent, purposeful actions to achieve them. I manage my finances wisely, making informed decisions that align with my long-term wealth vision. I am mindful and at peace.

Today, I cultivate a mindset of abundance, embracing the belief that there is always more than enough to go around. As wealth flows into my life, I use it as a tool for positive impact, contributing to the well-being of others and the betterment of the world. I am mindful and at peace.

I am the architect of my financial destiny, building a legacy of prosperity, generosity, and fulfillment. Every step I take is a deliberate stride toward the realization of my financial dreams. I am mindful and at peace.

I am on a journey to become wealthy, and I approach this path with determination, focus, and a relentless work ethic. Wealth creation is not just a goal but a mindset that I cultivate daily. I am mindful and at peace.

I am committed to expanding my financial knowledge, continuously seeking opportunities for growth, and making informed decisions that align with my vision of wealth. I embrace challenges as opportunities to learn and evolve, understanding that setbacks are temporary and can be valuable lessons in the journey toward wealth. I am mindful and at peace.

Today, I set clear and achievable financial goals, breaking them down into actionable steps that I can take consistently. I am resourceful, exploring various income generation and investment avenues, and I am open to adapting my strategies as the financial landscape evolves. I am mindful and at peace.

Today, I prioritize disciplined savings and wise financial management, laying the foundation for sustainable wealth accumulation. I surround myself with mentors and like-minded individuals who inspire and support my wealth-building journey. I am mindful and at peace.

Today, I use my growing wealth not only to enhance my own life but also to contribute positively to the lives of others and make a meaningful impact in the world. I am dedicated to the pursuit of financial abundance, and with each intentional step, I am becoming wealthier, more empowered, and closer to the realization of my financial aspirations. I am mindful and at peace.

I am a bastion of patience, navigating life's journey with a calm and unwavering demeanor. I understand that great things take time, and I trust in the process of growth and transformation. I am mindful and at peace.

Today, patience is my ally, a virtue that allows me to endure challenges with grace and resilience. In moments of uncertainty, I remain composed, knowing that patience is the key to unraveling the mysteries of time. I am mindful and at peace.

References

Maslach, C., & Leiter, M. P. (2016). Understanding the burnout experience: 1976–2016. In Research Companion to Organizational Health Psychology (pp. 295-311). Edward Elgar Publishing.

Stress Symptoms in Men: Physical and Psychological Signs https://www.verywellmind.com/recognizing-stress-for-men-2329008

Stress effects on the body https://www.apa.org/topics/stress/body
7 Simple Mindfulness Exercises That Can Reduce Stress ... https://www.self.com/story/best-mindfulness-exercises

Beware a Culture of Busyness https://hbr.org/2023/03/beware-a-culture-of-busyness

The Importance Of Setting Healthy Boundaries https://www.forbes.com/sites/forbescoachescouncil/2021/07/01/the-importance-of-setting-healthy-boundaries/

How To Delegate Effectively: 8 Strategies https://www.forbes.com/sites/allbusiness/2023/05/25/how-to-delegate-effectively-8-ways-to-make-the-most-of-your-teams-time-and-talent/

How to Stop Being a People-Pleaser (But Still Be You) https://psychcentral.com/health/tips-to-stop-being-a-people-pleaser

How Self-Care and Time-Management Go Hand-In-Hand https://www.delegated.com/blog/self-care-and-time-management

Mindfulness meditation: A research-proven way to reduce stress https://www.apa.org/topics/mindfulness/meditation

Why Single-Tasking Makes You Smarter https://www.forbes.com/sites/nextavenue/2013/05/08/why-single-tasking-makes-you-smarter/

Sleep Meditation Using Guided Imagery - HelpGuide.org https://www.helpguide.org/meditations/sleep-meditation-using-guided-imagery.htm
Top 10 morning routines of highly successful people - Ideas https://www.wework.com/ideas/professional-development/management-leadership/the-morning-routines-of-successful-people

Mindfulness for Your Health | NIH News in Health https://newsinhealth.nih.gov/2021/06/mindfulness-your-health

Nutritional psychiatry: Your brain on food - Harvard Health https://www.health.harvard.edu/blog/nutritional-psychiatry-your-brain-on-food-201511168626

Sleep Hygiene https://www.cci.health.wa.gov.au/[]/media/CCI/Mental-Health-Professionals/Sleep/Sleep---Information-Sheets/Sleep-Information-Sheet---04---Sleep-Hygiene.pdf

Want to Relax? Try Yoga https://www.nytimes.com/article/yoga-stress-relief.html

140 Daily Positive Affirmations For Men To Boost Self Esteem ... https://www.mentalhelp.net/blogs/140-daily-positive-affirmations-for-men/

Mindfulness can be a powerful conflict resolution tool https://www.peoplemanagement.co.uk/article/1741633/mindfulness-as-a-powerful-conflict-resolution-tool[]:[]:text=Resolving%20conflict,-Conflict%20is%20an&text=When%20a%20conflict%20arises%2C%20mindfulness,rather%20than%20knee%2Djerk%20react.

The Art of Zen Leadership | Future Leaders https://www.nrpa.org/parks-recreation-magazine/2019/may/the-art-of-zen-leadership/

The Power of Mindful Communication: Improving ... - LinkedIn https://www.linkedin.com/pulse/power-mindful-communication-improving-relationships

Men's Health Awareness: Why Vulnerability is a Strength https://organizations.headspace.com/blog/mens-health-awareness-why-vulnerability-is-a-strength:text=Being%20vulnerable%20can%20help%20us,flex%20our%20emotional%20intelligence%20muscles.

Active Listening: Techniques, Benefits, Examples https://www.verywellmind.com/what-is-active-listening-3024343

A Guide to Setting Better Boundaries https://hbr.org/2022/04/a-guide-to-setting-better-boundaries

A Zen Approach to Conflict Resolution https://greenleafcoach.com/2021/06/17/zen-approach-conflict-resolution/

Mindfulness for People Who Are Too Busy to Meditate https://hbr.org/2014/03/mindfulness-for-people-who-are-too-busy-to-meditate
Neuroscience Reveals the Secrets of Meditation's Benefits https://www.scientificamerican.com/article/neuroscience-reveals-the-secrets-of-meditation-s-benefits/

Evoking calm: Practicing mindfulness in daily life helps https://www.health.harvard.edu/blog/evoking-calm-practicing-mindfulness-in-daily-life-helps-202110142617

I Actually Tried Meditation for 30 Days–This Is What Happened https://www.success.com/i-actually-tried-meditation-for-30-days-this-is-what-happened/

How The Most Successful People Manage Stress https://www.forbes.com/sites/omaidhomayun/2021/06/01/how-the-most-successful-people-manage-stress/

A study on the relationship between mindfulness and work ... https://www.ncbi.nlm.nih.gov/pmc/articles/PMC9940765/

Reduce Stress: 8 Tips To Zen Your Workspace https://www.henryford.com/blog/2016/09/reduce-stress-8-tips-to-zen-your-workspace

What is Zen Meditation? Benefits & Techniques - Mindworks https://mindworks.org/blog/what-is-zen-meditation-benefits-techniques/
How to Start a Mindfulness Meditation Group https://www.tarabrach.com/starting-meditation-group/

What is Zen Meditation? Benefits & Techniques - Mindworks https://mindworks.org/blog/what-is-zen-meditation-benefits-techniques/
Treeleaf Zendo - Treeleaf Zendo, A Soto Zen Buddhist Sangha https://www.treeleaf.org/

How To Organize A Successful Meditation Retreat https://academy.wetravel.com/organize-successful-meditation-retreat
Most Famous Burnt Out Quotes that can Enlighten you [2024 Update]. https://kiiky.com/most-famous-burnt-out-quotes-that-can-enlighten-you/

The Power of Pause: Embracing Regular Breaks for Enhanced Productivity - TheRain.Dev. https://therain.dev/the-power-of-pause-embracing-regular-breaks-for-enhanced-productivity/

Business Management – Ascendance Academy. https://ascendanceacademy.in/question-category/ugcnetccommerce/organizational-behaviour/

Blog and News - Hope in Healing Therapeutic Services. https://www.hopeinhealingtherapy.com/blog/category/selfcare

Accountable Healthcare - Evoking calm: Practicing mindfulness in daily life helps. https://www.ahcstaff.com/evoking-calm-practicing-mindfulness/

Workplace Conflict Resources - BlueMediation. http://bluemediation.com/resources/

Top 10 morning routines of highly successful people - Ideas. https://www.wework.com/ideas/professional-development/management-leadership/the-morning-routines-of-successful-people

Breathing Labs – 7 Simple Mindfulness Exercises That Can Reduce Stress and Anxiety. https://www.breathinglabs.com/anxiety-management/7-simple-mindfulness-exercises-that-can-reduce-stress-and-anxiety/

Rediscovering meaning and purpose at work: The transpersonal psychology background of a burnout prevention programme – Erasmus University Rotterdam. https://pure.eur.nl/en/publications/rediscovering-meaning-and-purpose-at-work-the-transpersonal-psych-2
53 Great Teacher Affirmations That Keep the Mind Positive. https://elementaryassessments.com/teacher-affirmations/

Embracing Challenges On Your Spiritual Path - ourmindandbody.com. https://ourmindandbody.com/embracing-challenges-on-your-spiritual-path/

The Fiery Dance of Scorpio and Sagittarius: Embracing Passionate Compatibility - Coquette Woman. https://coquettewoman.com/index.php/scorpio-and-sagittarius-compatibility/

soul – Ticking With Purpose. https://www.tickingwithpurpose.com/tag/soul/

Mindfulness Quotes - K.A Luxe Media. https://kaluxemedia.com/2021/05/29/k-a-l-173/

Things we love: Those sneaky salamanders | Forest Preserve District of Will County. https://www.reconnectwithnature.org/news-events/the-buzz/things-we-love-those-sneaky-salamanders/

Meditation Vs Mindfulness: Differences And Similarities | primexaos. https://primexaos.com/meditation-vs-mindfulness-differences-and-similarities/

Pilates and Wellness for EVERY Body - The Pilates Center. https://www.thepilatescenter.net/blog/archives/08-2018

Are Gucci Loafers True To Size? – SizeChartly. https://sizechartly.com/are-gucci-loafers-true-to-size/

Calm Your Worried Mind With These Self-Soothing Techniques for Adults | Lifehacker. https://lifehacker.com/calm-your-worried-mind-with-these-self-soothing-techniq-1850208405

20 Ways to Improve Your Life Without Really Trying. https://www.onlygoodnewsdaily.com/post/20-ways-to-improve-your-life-without-really-trying

Battling Burnout: Finding Balance in a Hectic World - Develefy Consulting. https://develefy.com/blog/battling-burnout-finding-balance-in-a-hectic-world/

Bagodi, V. Exploring burnout and its consequences in DPsych trainee counselling psychologists using a mixed-method study. https://core.ac.uk/download/561047930.pdf

Employment Law - Pace Law Firm. https://pacelawfirm.comemployment-law/

Blind, K., Florez Ramos, E., & Fullea Carrera, E. (2018). CIFRA: Challenging the ICT Patent Framework for Responsible Innovation.

D3.2: Report on Assessment of Impact of proposed new Framings. https://core.ac.uk/download/288499251.pdf

Looking Good & Feeling Great At Any Age: Elle Macpherson's Secrets | mindbodygreen. https://www.mindbodygreen.com/articles/elle-macphersons-beauty-secrets

Dos and Don'ts When Making a SMART Goal (updated) - leadsbazaarllc.com. https://leadsbazaarllc.com/dos-and-donts-when-making-a-smart-goal-updated/

A Comprehensive Guide To Understanding Bioidentical Hormones | Ona's Natural. https://us.onasnatural.com/guide-to-bioidentical-hormones/

Some People Take Photo Manipulation Services | FitYes Fitness. https://www.fityesfitness.com/forum/wellness-forum/some-people-take-photo-manipulation-services

How to Reduce the Risks of Physical Inactivity + 20 Micro-activites you can do – Alkaline for Life. https://alkalineforlife.com/blogs/news/how-to-reduce-the-risks-of-physical-inactivity

Carla Konyk-Tulp on How Wildlife Can Improve Your Mental Health. https://www.dailyscanner.com/carla-konyk-tulp-on-how-wildlife-can-improve-your-mental-health/

17 Boundaries Quotes | Psych Central. https://psychcentral.com/health/quotes-healthy-boundaries

FAQ About The Pomodoro Technique. https://faqabout.me/iam/the-pomodoro-technique

101 simple calm-down strategies for kids to help them manage big emotions - Messy, Yet Lovely. https://messyyetlovely.com/simple-calm-down-strategies-for-kids/

Empower Others, Sustain Momentum

Now that you've equipped yourself with all the tools to conquer burnout and reclaim your life, it's time to pay it forward and guide other readers toward the same transformative journey.

By simply sharing your candid thoughts about this book on Amazon, you'll not only steer fellow burnout battlers in the right direction but also ignite their enthusiasm for overcoming this pervasive challenge. Thank you for extending your hand. The battle against burnout gains strength when we pass on our insights–and you're playing a pivotal role in that mission.

Scan this QR code to leave your review on Amazon.

How To Stop Burnout

Printed in Great Britain
by Amazon

39639912R00066